THESE OZARKS HILLS:
The First Five Years

THESE OZARKS HILLS:
The First Five Years

The Complete collection of episodes
from the radio series by

Marideth Sisco

VOLUME ONE

May, 2007
Through
May, 2012

Yarnspinner Press

P.O. Box 434
West Plains, MO 65775

This book is dedicated first to Kathleen Morrissey, who cooked up the whole idea of putting me and my stories on the radio, second to the staff of KSMU-FM, Public Radio in the Ozarks, and in particular Missy Shelton Belote and Jennifer Moore Davidson for shepherding me into the digital age (and putting up with me in the process), and finally to the people of the Ozarks, who have never failed to give me something curious, poignant and often hilarious to talk about.

Contents

Foreword
Frank L. Martin
Editor and Publisher
West Plains Daily Quill

You are holding a handbook on the Ozarks, part owner's manual, part travel guide, part map, and part almanac. Oh, and part gardener's diary.

The book is composed of installments in a series Marideth Sisco did for regional public radio. Most of the installments are stories about life in the Ozarks but some are musings, ponderings, reflections, and meditations on such subjects as friendship, the seasons and their changes, aging, and the pleasures of gardening.

There isn't any point in telling you much more about what is in the book or what I think about it. When you get past this forward you will find out for yourself.

What I can tell you is what I think about good stories, good storytellers, and, of course, Marideth.

Good stories are those that tell you something you don't know, or tell you what you already know in a more interesting and entertaining way. Good stories are not those collected with a project like a book in mind. Often, stories collected for a purpose contain embellishments that result in a loss of authenticity and honesty. Dishonesty has been the ruin of many books about the Ozarks.

Some stories about life in the Ozarks are as unique as their subject, but don't look for Lil' Abner, the Clampetts or Dogpatch: they were conjured in other places. They aren't genuine.

How stories come to storytellers and how they are crafted is a bit of a mystery. There is no making a list, then an outline, then fleshing something out. Good stories write themselves somehow, whole, like a jigsaw puzzle that arrives put together in substance and form when it comes out of the box. Marideth's arrive and are shared that way.

Marideth is a teller of good stories about the Ozarks because her eyes and ears are those of a native. Her gardener's hands are covered with Ozarks earth, her feet red from its clay--and from a little blood that leaked while she walked in the rocky places.

In the end, storytelling is a gift, often inherited. Marideth is gifted and comes from a long line of Ozarks tellers of Ozarks tales.

I call her Marideth here instead of by her last name because she was a newspaper reporter for me for many years. She was a good reporter. Her stories shined when I could get her to sit down and write them, when other stories didn't get in her way. She told me she is used to me as an editor, and that she asked me to write the forward because she knows I won't say anything good about her or her work that isn't true. I haven't.

Even so, the nature of our friendship is such that I haven't even mentioned to her, never mind complained, that after she delivered her manuscript to my desk so I could write this, dozens of sugar ants crawled out and began foraging. I won't ask whether she was working on the manuscript in the garden. Maybe it was lying next to where she was making bread and butter pickles.

A final thing about Marideth is that wherever she goes she collects friends along with her stories.

Most of us in the Ozarks are friendly that way. So, friends, get your hands in our soil and our clay on your feet.

Join us in These Ozarks Hills.

Frank L. Martin
Crow's Nest Farm
Peace Valley, Missouri
July 23, 2012

Acknowledgements

Long before this book was a thought in my mind, I was asked to help create a radio show, any kind of radio show, that would help the Missouri State University's West Plains Campus begin adding to the main campus's National Public Radio affiliate, KSMU-FM, a small bit of locally initiated programming.

I first sought to enlist the help of long-time friends Bill Oakley and Chris Rock, who had once been the mainstays of such local radio theater ventures as the Heart of the Ozarks Theater Company. They said they would. But there was no budget, no real studio apart from the noisy and often otherwise occupied public access television studio at the West Plains Civic Center, with no idea what kind of show it might be, other than 5 minutes, once a month, every month.

I tried interviewing local people and let them tell their stories. That worked, until the day a story was due and there was no interviewee available. So I just wrote something and recorded it myself. Thus began the show that became "These Ozarks Hills."

Every month has been an adventure; every story a revelation of something I didn't know or didn't know I knew. But mostly it's a divinely slapstick undertaking, wrestling unwieldy technology, making my hillbilly voice speak clearly and distinctly and my aging and ADD mind stay on point. My audience, my handlers at the station and the folks whose lives I've blabbed on about month after month have been endlessly kind and forgiving. I plan to keep on at this until I get tired of it, which might take a while.

Meanwhile, for everyone who listens, as well as everyone who conspires to keep me up and moving toward telling the good tale, I am forever in your debt. I owe special thanks to KSMU and its staff for hosting and helping foster this rattletrap endeavor; the facilities and technical support of the Media Arts Center where the show is recorded; Sarah Denton, my assistant, whose unfailing support and humor have made possible this and many other creative adventures; songwriting partner Robin Frederick for her guidance through the publishing sloughs and thickets; editor Carol McGinnis who relieved me of over 1,000 commas along with numerous other errors and omissions, and finally, the irrepressible Barbara Rosenblat of NATF, who taught me to be deliberate in my speech, sometimes in spite of all my Ozarks leanings toward the contrary.

Introduction

By Debra Granik & Jonathan Scheuer

Director and Executive Producer of the film "Winter's Bone"

Getting to know Marideth Sisco is a process of gradually discovering how many things she does extraordinarily well-- singing, writing songs, reporting, collecting folklore, teaching, crafting audio essays, writing creative fiction and nonfiction, for starters. This can be a bit disconcerting. Then you discover the ruling passion that holds it all together--Marideth is a gardener.

The themes that run through her other work, of harmony and of the particularity of individual lives and voices, the love of old customs and practices that mark the seasons, the determination to nurture real wisdom in spite of the persistence of ignorance and prejudice, the need to preserve natural resources, to use whatever is at hand to the best advantage, the zest for good jokes, including the ones that are on us--these are all facets of one gardener's approach to the challenge of making things grow in a modest patch of unforgiving soil.

You can't hurry a garden, and tending one teaches you not just patience, persistence, and the rewards of continual effort, but also the pleasures of slowing down, and really seeing and listening to the beauty of your surroundings, whatever they are. Reading these essays soothes me.

They remind me of thoughts and attitudes that are no longer commonly available, and are all the more precious for that. The process of learning from those who have come before us is itself an art, one that is fast fading in this age when we think we have access to everything through a few clicks of a computer mouse. Real wisdom, the kind that helps us to live better lives, can't be Googled, but it can be learned, and it can be found right here.

2007

MAY: First Installment

This is Marideth Sisco. I don't know if I'm quite as old as
These Ozarks Hills, but I'm a _bona fide_ Ozarks native. My *uci uHc ky*
mother's family, the Gentrys and Fergusons, were English
and Scotch and one Cherokee great-grandmother. They were
mostly Republicans, mostly storekeepers and postmasters
and a host of other shy and responsible people who love me
but who wish I would neither sing so loudly nor talk on the
radio.

My father's people, The Siscos, came up from New
Orleans to settle in Carroll County, Arkansas. They were
English and Spanish, mostly, and one Cherokee great-great-
grandmother. They were thrown out of Spain for trying to
overthrow the king. In America, with no king to overthrow,
they were forced to become sheriffs, auctioneers and orators,
mostly Democrats, who were apt to burst into song or
engage in high jinks at the least provocation.

Until they died, my parents maintained a lively and
fractious alliance between these factions and took great
delight in going to the polls every election to cancel each
other's votes.

Growing up in the Ozarks, moving away and coming
home, I've seen it from both sides, and I know it's not always
meant as a compliment when someone says, "You're not
from here, are you?"

You may have heard about the farmer who chided a man
who'd only lived here 20 years and said he was beginning to
feel like a native.

"You'll never be that," the farmer said

3

"Well, no," the man said, "but my children..."

"No," the farmer said.

"What? What do you mean?" the man protested. "They were born here."

"Well," the farmer said, "if your cat had kittens in the oven, would you call 'em biscuits?"

I cut my teeth on stories about bushwhackers and bank robbers. My Aunt Juanita told the story of visiting her sister Beebe when she lived in a house at Newtonia that had been the Union Army headquarters in the war, and how she went to sleep counting the bullet holes in the walls. Now it's a historic site. Then it was just Aunt Beebe's house.

I became a journalist because of those stories. When I wrote on the history of Thomasville, in Oregon County, Missouri, the folks at the history magazine Ozarks Watch asked to reprint it. But when they did, they took out all the stories about the people. They said that's not history. That's just folklore.

Well, as smart as that fella at that magazine was, and no matter how well I liked him, he was definitely not from here.

I recall he used to tell about going out to do fieldwork and being invited to these country people's houses for dinner, and he would laugh at the idea that someone could stir mustard and chop onions into mashed potatoes and call it a salad.

And I would be thinking, Well, sir, if it's all they have to eat and they have worked hard to get it and they're willing to share it with you, I figure they can by God call it anything they please.

But he was a good man, with good intentions, and he loved this place or he wouldn't have stayed on, and neither would his children. Maybe one of these days we'll quit calling them biscuits.

About ten years ago or so, we went back to Newtonia to see the old brick house where Beebe lived. The family who lived there had just mowed the lawn. And we all got a surprise, for we had lived with a mythology that said no African American people had ever lived in our area. But outside the iron pickets of the family cemetery, there was another cemetery with fieldstone markers without names or dates. That's where the slaves were buried, you see. They were outside the fence. They weren't from here.

You know, I'm just another hillbilly with an opinion. But at my age, I remember an Ozarks that is fast passing away. When this generation of people is gone, the stories we tell of this place may be all we have left of it.

Back in '91, some hikers touring the Alps found a man who had been frozen in ice for more than 5,000 years. On his skin were tattooed acupuncture points, marks made 3,000 years before the Chinese invented it. And we call it experimental medicine. If we hadn't found these fragments of a man, we'd never have known that.

Fragments. Sometimes that's all we have, like pottery shards giving us clues to lost civilizations. Here in the Ozarks, though, there's still a unique and sometimes quite peculiar culture very much alive, just waiting to be explored. In the essays that follow, that's just what we'll be doing.

Author's Note:

It was an ambitious undertaking, given that although I had considerable experience at interviewing and storytelling, technical expertise was a whole other thing. I scrambled to find a workable field recorder, but with no budget, I was adrift. Finally I hit upon a website, "Transom" which had some good info on budget recorders. I chose a Sony minidisk recorder and a small condenser mic, available used on eBay. But I didn't have enough sense to practice with it before going out on my first interview. As a result, much of what I recorded was worthless, with the mic too far away or voices drowned out by wind or car noises. I ended up with only scraps, and even those are now unavailable because I inadvertently murdered the Sony shortly thereafter by inserting a live "Line In" into the "Line Out" plug, frying the circuits.
What follows here is that first interview, what was salvagable, in text form. It does neither the story nor the storyteller justice. Such are audio arts as practiced by the novice (or possibly by chimpanzees).

JUNE: The Rose Rustler

Hello. This is Marideth Sisco for These Ozarks Hills. Around here, a person can sometimes provoke a suspicious look when they say the word "preservation." In the Ozarks, it can mean many different things. One person might think you're talking about putting up peaches. Another might suspect you're out to tell them what to do on their back forty.

To some folks, though, preservation just means latching hold of the things that are precious before they're lost and gone. Some folks do it as a hobby. Others are pretty darn serious. Mary Lou Price of Ava, Missouri, is one of the latter.

Mary Lou scouts old cemeteries and home places, looking for those old roses that people used to pass down among families. They smell wonderful, but they've mostly been replaced by hybrids that are long on bloom but short on aroma. When she finds one of the old-timers, she takes home a cutting and attempts to persuade it to root. At last count, she had rescued between 35 and 40 old rose varieties. But she doesn't call herself a rose rescuer. She says she's a rose rustler.

I asked her to tell me how to collect an antique rose.

Mary Lou: It starts with a county map that shows all the cemeteries in the county. I color in the cemetery markings on the map. Then we load up a bucket, shears and a potato fork, in case there's enough to get a decent root cutting without harming the plant. If not, the shears are for taking actual stem cuttings to bring back."

Marideth: "Tell me how you make a stem cutting."

Mary Lou: "Usually, I look for something that is not real woody. Maybe it came from last year's growth, has a little bit of green to it. And it needs to be at least the length of a pencil. And you would cut the tip of it off and bury it in some moist soil. I like to put it in a flower pot and set it under my porch where it's somewhat shaded. It gets a little dab of light. Just keep it moist and with any luck, you'll have a rose in a few months."

Marideth: "You just ignore it, huh?"

Mary Lou: "Pretty well. Just water it down. Well, I go out every day and look at it."

Marideth: "You talk to it?"

Mary Lou: "Yes. There's one not very far away if you wanted to go see how it's done. The old moss rose I was telling you about earlier. We can go where it came from and I wanted to get a little bit of that rose to share with a friend of mine."

And so off we went to a cemetery in an undisclosed location where we rustled a rose. Preservation. Sometimes it's peaches. Sometimes it's roses. And sometimes it's someone to be thankful for like Mary Lou Price, the Rose Rustler.

JULY: Live Audio Theater in the Ozarks

I know many people think of the Ozarks as a laid back place to settle down. But for people who work in radio drama, West Plains becomes a real hot spot for at least one week of the year. It's not just the temperature, although it does happen at the end of June. That's when West Plains plays host to the National Audio Theatre Festival. It's a gathering of the best and brightest in all the audio arts. From voice actors such as Jeff Hedquist, Simon Jones and Barbara Caruso, recording engineers such as Tom Lopez, Henry Howard and NPR's Renee Pringle to Grammy-winning record producer Paul Reuben and Academy-Award nominee Randy Thom of Skywalker Studios. They have all come to West Plains except for Randy.

Randy was on a very tight schedule at the time, what with all the Harry Potter and Pixar movies for which he was providing sound. He couldn't appear in person, but he listened in and provided a critique after attendees set up microphone arrays and attempted to collect the best sample of the sound of a helicopter landing. He appeared via conference call and answered many questions.

There were also workshops in writing for the spoken word, voice acting, production techniques, computer software, sound effects, all the things that make radio, well, radio... all mixed in with a healthy dose of fun. One of the microphone samples that Randy reviewed, for instance, was recorded on an iPod mounted face down under a rock on the landing pad. He said he was surprised by how bad it wasn't.

Meanwhile, Dwight Frizzell and Michael Henry were putting together a sound composition in the theatre involving Indian flute, the helicopter, and a couple of Warthog A-10 fighter jets from Whiteman Air Force Base, near Kansas City.

At the same time, out in the lobby, Rhiana Yazzie, part of the Native American Radio Theatre group, was worrying over sound effects for her play "Peach Seed" while the voice actors were rehearsing their parts inside. I asked Rhiana how that was coming along.

Rhiana: "Well, today, for the Peach Seed, we had our first rehearsal, and tonight we're working on sound effects. So we're putting together all the cues and everything that's going to be in it: wind gusts, chopping of trees, fires...I think it's going to be a late night."

Outside, Charles Potter was busy creating those sound effects. "Charles, how's it going?" I asked.

Charles: "We're recording backgrounds for a scene where a cavalry charge is in the script. So we have a bunch of guys. They're all going to be charging by this surround-sound microphone to create the sense that we're right in the middle of the trail as the cavalry charges by."

The week ended with a two-hour non-stop performance before a live studio audience...just like it was done in the old days, but with much better toys. All in all, it made for a rip-roaring week of audacious audio antics right here in these Ozarks Hills.

Author's Note:

In the previous essay, sound recordings of interviewees were captured by Diane Ballon, a NATF staffer. The narrative was recorded by me on the media center's Marantz recorder, whose operating manual was just a bit shorter than volume One of the Encyclopedia Britannica, or so it seemed. I managed to punch the right button at least once. In the interview that follows, I carried the Marantz out to Rick Cochran's house, where Judy Domeny joined us for an evening of music. The recording quality was better due to a good machine. The sound card has since become one with the universe. One of the songs recorded that night has since been recorded on the Blackberry Winter album, "In These Ozarks Hills."

AUGUST: An Elusive Bird, the Ballad Singer

This month I've been out on the trail of a very elusive bird, the Ozarks ballad singer. They've gotten kind of hard to come by, these singers of the old songs that tell the stories of the past to the future, reminding of us of who we are and where we come from. But I found one and got her to sing a little for us. Judy Domeny spends her weekdays teaching art to school children in Rogersville, Missouri, and some of her weekends, believe it or not, being an auctioneer. And a pretty darn good one.

(Clip of Judy Domeny hosting an auction)
But her real love is for the old ballads, and she's been singing them for a long time. I wondered how her interest began.

Judy: "I found a book of folk songs and could see that I could play them. That was the first thing that interested me. I could play the songs in that book. And then I got intrigued by the stories, and also my dad knew some of them. He would sing them; he learned some of them as a kid and I thought that was ancient history if he knew them as a kid...So for the fun of it I was learning these songs. I was intrigued about queens and kings and Indians and cowboys and murderers so I...I just learned these songs. And then I started playing them out at Silver Dollar City and just have continued to play, and they have been a source of joy for me. And it's funny, I don't remember names, I don't remember dates very well. But I can remember a long-winded ballad. Put it to music and I can remember every word of it. I have a natural inclination to learn those ballads."

Sisco: "Surely people have asked you why you sing so many sad songs, but I guess most of the old songs are sad, aren't they? Why do you think the sad songs were so popular back then?"

Domeny: "Some of these songs stayed alive because if you were out here working this Ozarks rocky ground and you had ten kids tugging at your dress and you were having tto scrub on a washboard, weed the garden and the kitchen and the washboard and the kids were your life as a woman, I think maybe singing about a queen that got killed over in England would make you feel a little bit better about your laden life. I think it would. I think not only was it entertainment but you could say, 'Well at least I've got it better than she does.'"

Then I asked Judy if she'd sing something special, and she picked one of my favorites from the May Kennedy McCord Collection. "He came from his palace grand, and he came to my cottage door..." went the lyrics.
Oh, those old, sad songs. Love gone wrong, death come soon or sudden, the twist of fate. The stories of a rough and rocky path through These Ozarks Hills.

SEPTEMBER: Polly Langston

I'd like to tell you about Polly Langston. Polly was a poor little orphan girl who was befriended by a doctor from Marshfield, Missouri, while he was on a trip to New Orleans. She only spoke a few words of Spanish; and it was believed she came from Cuba. He took her home to his wife and son, where she became a member of the family. But then came that great tornado, the Marshfield cyclone of 1880 that killed more than a hundred people, and the doctor's family was not spared. Let's let West Plains historian, Dorotha Reavis, pick up the tale from that morning when volunteers from surrounding communities came to search for survivors.

Reavis: They heard what they thought was a baby cry "Mama, oh Mama," and it was Polly. She was near Dr. Bradford, and they found that he was dead. They finally located Mrs. Bradford. She had been blown out in the field and she was so badly bruised that she was almost beyond recognition. But Polly knew her and was comforted.
"But after that she just kept saying, 'Hey Ma! Where's Pa?' and this really disturbed Mrs. Bradford, who finally decided to send Polly to West Plains to her daughter, who was married to Thomas Jefferson Langston. After that Polly was so afraid of storms that every time she heard thunder she would begin to cry out and just have a fit. And they'd have to get a heavy quilt and cover Polly so that she couldn't hear the thunder so much, and she was comforted that way.

14

"Polly, when she was a teenager, had been taught to sing. And she had a favorite hymn that was called, "How Firm the Foundation" that she would sing quite frequently. And when she sang she insisted that someone in the family go to the piano and play for her.

"Now Mrs. Langston was host to the Ladies' Aid Society that met at her house regularly. Polly was always there and would listen to the ladies talking. And after they would leave, Polly would have a conversation with herself. She would say, 'Well goodbye Mrs. Smith. It was awfully nice having you. Oh, the cream was delicious.'

"Polly was just so loved by the family and not only was she really liked by the family but everyone in West Plains loved her. The Langston family lived on what is now Langston Street, across from Roberson Drago Funeral home, and Polly spent a lot of time out on the front porch and would take time to talk to people as they would pass by. So she became really popular all over Howell County and was much respected and loved by the citizens of our area. Polly was born in 1867 and in 1920, almost 53 years later, she died. And the family loved her so much they couldn't think of anything but to take her to Oak Lawn Cemetery and bury her in the Langston burial plot. Polly has her own tombstone that says Polly, 1867- 1920."

Sisco: It's an interesting tale with an interesting twist that made Polly's death noteworthy in newspapers nationwide. You see, Polly was a parrot, one of the more exotic birds to pass through These Ozarks Hills.

OCTOBER: Grandpa Henry

It's fall in the Ozarks. The days are getting shorter, the nights colder. Frost is creeping into the valleys, and owls want to know who cooks for you? We go out to see the colors and instead sometimes see ghosts. For these hills are old. Some say the oldest in America. Thinking about that sent me out in search of someone who remembered someone who remembered somebody still older, someone who got here a long time before we did. Someone such as Carol Silvey's Grandpa Henry.

Silvey: "My great-great-great grandfather came on the Trail of Tears, the infamous Cherokee march. After having crossed the Mississippi, they came across to Rolla. Grandpa Henry and eleven other young people decided they were not going to follow their elders to the Indian territory, and so they came south. They came down and spent the winter at Rainbow Springs...in the cave just above it. The other eleven chose to go on in the spring. Grandpa Henry decided to stay, and he stayed in Ozark County all his life."

Sisco: "Just how old was he, anyhow?"

Silvey: "He lived to be, according to his records, 105. We have not found records that prove that to be the fact. They don't prove that he was quite that elderly when he died, but we like the thought that we're from long-lived people so we kind of like that story as well."

Sisco: "So, he lived long enough that your father knew him?

16

Silvey: "He took my dad fishing. My dad was his favorite of his heirs, it seems. And Dad said you didn't know what hunting and fishing were until you went with Grandpa Henry. He was stealthy. He was accurate. He was committed. I recall dad telling stories about Grandpa Henry taking him fishing. According to Dad, he made a sound one day and Grandpa Henry got really upset and didn't take him fishing again for a long time. He said, 'All I did was say, 'Grandpa, do you think...' And he said, 'That's all I got out.' So, he took his fishing very seriously. Not his work, however. He just kind of wandered around and lived off the people and off of the land. He did a little bit of blacksmithing, just enough, and he lived in a hut that I saw as an adult. He had hollowed out a piece of ground, probably not any more than ten-by-ten feet. He had put kind of a lean-to of saplings and boards over it and that's where he spent his later years. Grandpa Henry was not a hard worker by any means. He hunted and fished and floated. He'd be gone for long periods of time and he would come back to the family and indicate to them that he had been visiting relatives who obviously were in the Indian territory at that point."

Sisco: That was Grandpa Henry. It is ghosts such as his that walk These Ozarks Hills. And he was just the ghost I was looking for.

Carol Silvey is a professor of history, the retired director of development for Missouri State University and now, the head of the West Plains office for the Community Foundation of the Ozarks. She is the great-great-great granddaughter of Grandpa Henry.

Author's note:

It was at this point, some six months after starting the series, that I abruptly ran out of people to interview. It's not that no one else had an interesting story; it's that they either didn't want to tell it just then, or they had gone to Texas for the holidays, or they had some other lame excuse, like being in the hospital or something. And I was on deadline. So I just wrote something out of my own story and delivered it. And people seemed to take to it well.

And so the series at this point began to take on a life of its own, supplemented by my own long history of storytelling – both the listening to and the telling of – what we in the Ozarks refer to as "Windies."

Truth is, after Christmas, I got a few more interviews with some interesting folks. I about decided the previous stories were just a stopgap. But no. Sooner or later, I'd go down the path of no return. A word of caution: Soon it'll be time to batten down the hatches. There's a world of Windies ahead.

NOVEMBER: To Be Thankful

Like many of you, I went traveling over the Thanksgiving holiday. I went down south to the land of cotton and rice and long, straight highways. On the way down, I didn't know the roads, so all my attention was on the map. But on the way back I knew the road. Everything on local radio was canned or bad for my blood pressure, and I was coming back from days of long conversations with people I've known and who've known me for a long time.

So I was replaying those conversations in my head. We talked about the struggle to find thankfulness in the wake of Katrina, ill health, children coming home from long distances and longer estrangements and those still struggling to find their way.

We grieved the passing of loved ones and the vast sadness that is now the Gulf Coast and the city of New Orleans. So much of what was precious now scattered to the winds.

But then Wilma made her father's famous apple pie. I made Aunt Juanita's famous home made noodles, Brenda candied the yams, Wanda made a toast, and we took a healthy dose of good food, good wine, and great stories of days gone by.

We laughed long, cried a little, and found our way into the spirit of the day with pumpkin pie on the side. Good medicine, indeed.

Brenda said that while we may all look like we've been through the mill, our voices are still those same young voices we've always known that laugh and joke and wonder what the big deal is about getting old anyway.

That was some return trip, crossing those barren fields, threading the strings of tiny towns where farmers recuperated from the holiday feast while wondering what their wives and kids were spending on Black Friday in Little Rock or Memphis or Jonesboro and if they'd have enough coin for their dreams.

People are worried these days, especially in the farmlands. This whole country seems to have been on a long trip down a lonely road of late, and if there is an end in sight, nobody is telling us about it. Even our planet home doesn't seem all that safe anymore.

All the more reason, I think to take time, not just on a special day but every time we get the chance to give thanks for what's important to us, just so we don't forget.

Me, for instance: I'm thankful for my health, what there is of it, and for the people who love me enough to help me make better choices. I'm thankful for my family and for yours. Don't ever take them for granted. Years pass, and so do people, and the older you get the fewer people remember that your voice is still young and carefree.

I'm thankful for the ties of friendship like those renewed this weekend. And the ones right here on the air during last month's fundraiser when voices from my past called in to donate to this station. What a fine day that was.*

I'm thankful for those people and for the people I don't even know who make my life better by doing their jobs well...not for applause or for rewards but because it's the right thing to do. We don't ever thank them enough.

Of course I finally made it back to the end of the flatlands where the road begins to twist and twine its way up towards the Ozarks, back where the air is sweeter and folks don't have an accent.

I hope your holiday was as warm and heart-filling as mine was, and if you didn't get the chance to say thank you enough to those who make your life better and fuller and richer, there is still time.

Giving thanks: may it never go out of season.

This comment was in response to an on-air fundraising effort at KSMU-FM, Springfield, Missouri, a National Public Radio affiliate.

DECEMBER: The Longest Night

Ever since we first began to walk on our hind legs, humans have pondered the behavior of this strange, wobbly planet that wanders its tipsy way through space. Rolling and weaving like a top, it gives us summer and winter, the seasons, the solstices and the holidays that have gathered around them. Among these is the passing of the longest night, and how its darkness generates the hope of the light to come. What an incredible metaphor and how deeply it speaks to us. It has given us traditions that go back thousands of years, from the Ramadan of the Muslims, the Hannukah of the Jews, to the many and varied celebrations of Christmas.

Oh, we may huff and puff over what a Christmas tree means, and whether it's a Christian symbol or a pagan one. But whether a Christmas tree, the menorah's candles or the glow of the Yule log, they all bring light to the long winter's night.

Down here in the Ozarks, most of us have come to that long winter's night with a good helping of memories of seasons, holidays, loved ones present and past and stories to share by the fire and warm our hearts while the cider and good company take care of the rest. Here's one to add to that batch.

When I was just a little bitty kid, I was very worried about Christmas. I thought Santa wouldn't be able to come and see me at all. I had been fretting about it for some time because we were living in this big, drafty, old house that had been the town hotel in Butterfield, Missouri. We were living

22

in just the rooms that we could heat in the winter with an old wood stove, and there was no fireplace. I could see that the chimney was just up on the wall with just a little bitty hole for the stovepipe, and how in the world would Santa get down out of there? Well, he couldn't.

Well, Christmas Eve came, and there I was, fretting about Santa. All of a sudden, I heard this big ho-ho-ho, and the front door opened. By golly, in walked Santa Claus... tall, and all in red and with the white beard and everything. I had never seen anyone so tall except Leonard, my aunt Juanita's new husband, and he was gone off to town somewhere. Santa came in and set me up on his knee and reached in his sack and pulled out these very cool toy telephones that really rang and talked to each other, and these little cars and trucks, and candy, and, well, I just don't know what all, I could hardly look at the toys, because there he was, big as life. Bigger.

Then Santa Claus explained that, what with the chimney problem and all, he couldn't land on the roof and he had to land in the yard, which was tricky. He didn't want to be seen by anybody, so he really had to get going. He sat me down, stood up, and off down the hall and out the front door he went.

Well, hey, I was nobody's fool. If Santa Claus was parked in the yard and if I hurried, I could see me some reindeer. So I was off down the hall like a shot, right behind him, with my mom and dad and aunt Juanita calling after me. Well, I guess Santa realized I was on his heels, 'cause he made a left turn at the front door and tore off around the side of the house at a dead run. Now, I don't know where he put his sleigh, but I do know that's where we'd put the woodpile.

Now I don't really remember this part of the story, but I'm told that I when I came back to the kitchen, my eyes full of wonder, I said:

"You know, when Santa Clause cusses, he sounds just like Uncle Leonard."

I swear they told that story on me every Christmas until I was the only one of them left, and now I tell it on myself. It's what we do on the long winter nights to warm our hearts and make the winter go quicker and bring back the light. And I guess this old wobbly planet listens, because it's already leaning back toward the sun, and mornings are getting a little longer every day. Whatever your tradition, it's easy to see that when we went looking for a holy season, this was a good place to put it. May this holiday season find you well and happy, your days lengthening and the light in your life strengthening.

2008

JANUARY: The Broadfoot Collection

Almost 100 years ago, Lennis Broadfoot, a Shannon County boy of Cherokee heritage who had a passion for drawing, went west to seek his fortune. He became a successful commercial artist. But in the Great Depression, he left his family behind in California and returned to the Ozarks to to draw the people from whom he'd come. The result? Almost 300 drawings, mostly in charcoal but a few in oil, of a generation that was fast passing away. As he drew, he also wrote down the subjects' stories.

Today, those drawings and the stories reside in the Harlin Museum in West Plains. They're the basis of programs such as History Works, where actors depict the Broadfoot characters and bring their stories to life. Since this is the print version of the tales, let's look at some of those drawings as we read the stories the subjects chose to tell as their portraits were being drawn.

Ellen Boxx: "My husband Jake works around the saw mills where they manufacture lumber or at anything else he can get to do. I have even made all the furniture I have in my house.

Mary Rasor: "We've got our own workshop. Make about everything we use, even to this furniture in our house. We always had to work in the fields til the summer's work was done and the crops laid by and then go to the old spinning wheel and loom and make our clothes.

Jess Thompson: "I'll bet I can kill more squirrels with rocks than most fellers can with a gun. Now boys, boy, I just wish you could see all of them in a pile that I've knocked out of these trees with rocks.

Lissie Moffat: "I'm 85 years old and was married when I was pretty young and raised my family of four girls. I got a cow, some chickens and a dog. And I've raised my own garden. It's mighty nice to have all these things that you've raised yourself and can sit and spit in your own fireplace in the wintertime when the ground is all covered with snow and enjoy life.

Vina Boxx "Henry splits clapboards and kivvers houses and I keep the old spinning wheel humming to help make a living and it seems like it keeps us both busy to keep the wolf from the door and keep going. Me and Henry have always been hard-working critters and while we hain't got no finery, we hain't starvin' neither. And we'll get by somehow.

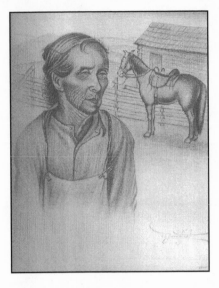

Margaret Swiney: "I have as midwife waited on more than 400 maternity cases and delivered that many babies to this world. Sometimes, I would have 10 miles to go with nothing but a trail to follow through the hills and so dark you could hardly see your hand before you. And many times, it'd be raining and freezing and my shoes would freeze fast to the saddle stirrups before I'd get there. They were all poor people. Sometimes I got a little pay but most of the time, no pay at all, but they needed me so bad and I couldn't say no.

Miller Bell: "Sometimes I think I could sit on a sack of taters and run a better government than some of them do. These duck-billed, beer-bellied politicians come around at election time, making their soapbox speeches and telling us old humpy farmers how they're going to take the whole works apart and see what makes it tick. Every time those greasy-tongued liars puts in a new wheel, it's one that grinds a new kink in our legs and a hump on our backs. I can see that if

30

we ever get anywhere, we've got to do something besides set on a sack of taters and talk.

Robert Shiffler: "I done fine til those durn old automobiles come in and robbed me of my profession and drove me out of business. Makes me mad every time I look at a durn old car. They're the very thing that has bankrupted the world and put people on the bum. They're just a fast streak of waste and an extravagance that's caused all the world to go speed-crazy and do nothing but burn up time and money. What a nasty mess of monkey business they have got this world into. But there you go and where we're going to wind up?

Marideth: Stories to ponder on a winter's evening. Times have changed a great deal. But then, not so much.

FEBRUARY: Goodbyes and Omens

Last week, I went down out of these hills, down to Mississippi to say goodbye to a friend. It seems like I've been doing that a lot lately, but I guess it's like the fellow says - the older you get, the more it seems like you're either plantin' someone or getting' planted. So I guess I shouldn't complain, having avoided the latter so far. But I came back from the trip feeling uneasy.

This was the first time I had returned to the Gulf Coast since the nightmare that was Katrina, and I wasn't looking forward to it, afraid that too many of the things I remembered would be gone. Many of them were.

Oh, the casinos were back and doing a land-office business. Motels were open, and favorite restaurants, although not always in the same locations where they used to be. MacElroys Restaurant had moved all the way from Gulfport over to Ocean Springs. But we tracked it down and had dinner there. It was nice to see they're rebuilding Jeff Davis's house, and the art museum was going back up, though it was still just a shell.

The saddest to see were the long stretches of beach highway that had been lined with homes, now just sand pocked with debris and an occasional concrete front porch or a few brave daffodils. People were apparently reluctant to rebuild on the water just yet. And I suppose some of the people who lived there may not have survived.

But the Gulf is always a survival story, always a work in progress. She has always known storms, always weathered them. She even has names for all of them. People talk about

Ivan and Jorge and Frederick and most legendary of all, Camille. Everyone has a story to tell about her.

Here's a curious thing, though, that may speak to something larger than hurricanes, in these times. Now, there is a storm these Gulf Coast residents won't name. The only time I heard the word Katrina was when I said it myself, and when I said it, always a silence followed. And then someone would say, "Well, after the Storm..." or "That was Before the Storm..." or "We lost all that in the Storm." They wouldn't call her by name. It was like they were afraid of invoking an evil presence.

After a couple of trips past the wounded live oaks, with the Spanish moss still torn and tattered, past the barren sand where communities once thrived, over the beach highway that was still, two years later, almost entirely a construction zone, I, too, stopped using the K word.

Sometimes a storm is more than a storm. Sometimes it's a metaphor for the things we endure that are beyond our capacity to take in. Maybe we read the newspaper and have to ask, as I heard in a restaurant here at home, "Is this a new mass killing at a college or are they still talking about that other one?" Or we read an essay describing the fall of an ancient empire and we suddenly lose our place in time and have to stop and say, "Wait, are they talking about then, or is this about now?"

Or when the Ozarks weather shifts from ice to flower buds to ice again, and spring is caught in the deadly flux of climate confusion and official sources assure us everything will be fine, so long as we pay no attention to Al Gore.

Sometimes a storm is more than a storm. Sometimes it's something you're unable to name, but you can see the signs. Everyone is feeling uneasy these days, but down in Mississippi and along the Gulf Coast, there is the storm with no name. It's left a mark that runs three states wide, a hundred miles deep inland. People on the Gulf have been reading those signs, and I saw them, too. The Gulf is a beautiful place, and people have worked hard to put things back in order, even to carving beautiful sculptures from some of the ruined trees. They're patching up the highway, the daffodils are blooming, the casinos are back in business. But nobody is building homes by the water. Just like they don't call the storm by name, like they don't really think they've seen the worst of it yet.

MARCH: The Kreighs, Remembered

These days, when we look for a weather forecast, we think of Doppler radar, storm chasers, and high-tech, up-to-the-minute information. We forget that not so long ago and not so far out in rural areas, weather forecasting was a different story.

Like many an Ozarker, I grew up on the wise words of C.C. Williford, iconic weatherman on KWTO in Springfield. But out here in West Plains, it was hard to hear C.C. unless you parked your car out on a hilltop, like some did to listen to St. Louis Cardinal games. So in 1949, at KWPM Radio, Bob Neathery decided to create his own local weather broadcast. He hired the fella who took the local weather statistics for the National Weather Service to do it. That fellow was Greyhound Bus Station manager P.S. Kreigh and his wife Julia.

Like the Krieghs, those broadcasts are long gone. But Laurel Thompson and John Dedecker, broadcasters who once worked at KWPM with P.S. Kreigh and his wife, remember them. And they sat down with me recently to share some of those memories. Now I'd like to share them with you

John: "CC Williford would always talk about his garden and what was going on around the area, and he would incorporate that in his weather reports. Mr. Kreigh just emulated what CC Williford had been doing and that's what you heard on the air."

35

Laurel: "For many, many years, they had a little one-lung amplifier down in the basement at their home, and they would actually do their reports from their basement. I think he took a lot of pride in being THE weather observer for West Plains and the vicinity, and he well should have."

John: "He never got a salary. He got paid a little bit in later years, so much for each report."

Laurel: "Once, he actually contributed to one of the fellas at the radio station losing his job. This fella hadn't been on the air at KWPM very long, and he introduced Mr. Kreigh and you could hear papers shuffle. Mr. Kreigh was there but didn't have his headset on, so the fella didn't really know what to do but to introduce him again. He went through the routine of the introduction and still, all they could hear was the shuffling of paper. After a third time, Albert forgot to turn off his own mic and said out loud, 'I wonder what's the matter with the old so-and-so now.' And in less than 30 minutes,' he was fired.
John, do you remember the morning Mr. Kreigh choked on a corn flake?"

John: "Yeah. He'd say a couple or three words and then he'd have to cough."
Laurel: "Not only cough but gag."

John: "Oh yeah. And this one morning, he could get just a couple of words out and then (cough). And I mean he just carried on this coughing. His report was supposed to be five minutes but that particular morning, it took him about ten minutes and every two or three words (cough). The next morning, he came on the air and said, 'I have to apologize for yesterday, but I was choked on my corn flakes.'"

Laurel: "Mrs. Kreigh, I think the older she got, the more she was really intrigued by the almanac. I distinctly remember one morning that Margaret and I had been out to a little patch we had established. For the first time ever, we had planted potatoes. We'd gotten out there about daylight and as we left, we heard Mrs. Kreigh saying that that day was a barren day in the almanac and not to plant anything that would develop in the ground. And then lo and behold, we had the awfulest gob of potatoes you ever saw in your life and a lot of them weighed over a pound a piece.

"I think the Kreighs really became icons. They were so unique. Everybody loved them. They'd laugh about some of the things that happened and thoroughly enjoy a lot of the things that did happen on the air...and it was live."

John: "Their equipment was downstairs in the basement next to the washer and dryer. There were a lot of broadcasts where you'd hear the slush of the washing machine going. And she wouldn't turn it off."

Laurel: "There were times the phone would ring and particularly Mrs Kreigh would pick up the phone and say, 'I'm on the radio now. I can't talk to you. Call back in a little bit.' And clunk. It was live and in color."

John: "That was the Ozarks at that time. A lot of people, if they wanted to know what the weather was going to be like, thought they had to tune in and hear Mr. Kreigh's weather. I can remember my grandmother. She thought if Mr. Kreigh said it was going to be a cool morning and you needed a jacket, you'd better get a jacket out."

Laurel: "Sometimes, Mr. Kreigh had some extra help like a little bit of water poured in the rain gauge. The observatory was inside a chain-link fence, but it wasn't locked and it was a great opportunity for high school kids who didn't have enough to do to see if they could modify the forecast. And they did."

John: "Like Laurel said, they were icons in the area. They definitely were. They were the weather."

APRIL: A Fur Trapper Speaks of his Trade

This is Marideth Sisco for These Ozarks Hills. You know, as I get older, I'm afraid I'm getting a little bit opinionated. We can get comfortable in our beliefs if we're not challenged, especially on things far removed from our daily lives. I once heard a talk by an expert, meaning he was from out of town, who said that farmers should get away from their tractors and get back to the mattock and hoe. I figure about ten minutes with a mattock in our rocky soil would change his mind. Then I found out he wrote that book on his computer in his New York City apartment. I guess it's Ok to live in your own world. When it gets troublesome is when we try to make everybody live just like us.

This week, I visited with a man whose profession is nearly as old as the world itself. Some people think he should give it up. He says we've already changed the world too much to pretend we're not a part of the ecosystem. In the wild, the human is the last surviving large predator as well as the one charged with stewardship. Kenny Wells of Salem was recently inducted into the Missouri Fur Trappers Hall of Fame. Here was our conversation:

Wells: We harvest a renewable natural resource just like if you were logging or anything else. We sometimes are misunderstood, but there's a very definite need: there are more animals than the land can sustain. They die of disease, starvation. That's a whole lot more cruel than harvesting them. There has to be a balance. That's where we as trappers are probably more conservation-minded than any other

39

group of individuals because a trapper has to figure out the animals' habits, what they want to eat, how they live. We're connected to their lives."

Sisco: "That makes sense to me. Sounds more like a way of life than an occupation."

Wells: "That's true. We trap from November 15 to January 20 each year, but we have to be a trapper 365 days a year. We may not be out there setting the traps, but we have to stay in tune with nature. And that never stops.
"I'm 59 and I started trapping in earnest when I was about ten years old. Trapped on my grandpa's farm, was interested in trapping as a child. And I just kept working at it, had the old timers show me things, kind of a self-taught trapper. Love nature, love the outdoors."

Sisco: "Is trapping the major part of your livelihood?"

Wells: "I'm a farmer also. Me and my wife work the farm together. She helps me trap, too. We've enjoyed the sport of trapping ever since we've been married. Both born and raised right here around Salem.

Sisco: "Where do you think the controversy comes from, is it just folks who live in town and think meat comes from the supermarket?"

Wells: "Well, yes, I think a lot of people don't understand it. They think, 'Well, you just harvest the fur because you get money out of it.' That's the least part of it. We trap raccoon, otter, beaver, muskrat, mink, coyote, fox, bobcat. There's a few badger but not very many. This is just the edge of their range."

Sisco: "I understand you had to cross swords with the feds here a while back to get the regulations straightened out."

Wells: "Yes, in 1982, the National Park Service, through a change in regulation decided we could no longer trap on the Ozark National Scenic Riverways. At that time, we had to take them to court and won our right to trap. I think it was pretty important. But this is what happens. We get people far removed from the outdoors and they're in positions of authority and then that creates problems because they don't really realize the impact to people's lifestyle they're making when they make these regulations. It's important for them to understand us. Not everybody's a trapper. There's people that don't like to trap. I realize that. That's fine but I don't know that they should tell me that I can't. People want to go back like it was before any human activity was ever in the wilderness. That isn't going to happen. It's too late. Everything we do affects life in the wild now. We have to take the responsibility to keep a very delicate balance. We need to understand wildlife and our effect on the natural world. Once you put your thumb on the scale of nature. It never returns."

MAY: Old Time Music

Whenever you mention old time music in this part of the hills, you can stir up some memories that go back a long way. Some recall the folklorists and song collectors such as Max Hunter and May Kennedy McCord. Others remember the sweet fiddle tunes of Art Galbraith, Saturday nights at Souder Store or wandering down the back roads of Arkansas, trying to find Jimmy Driftwood's barn.

For us wandering souls, it brings back all those old times we gathered round to warm our hearts before the television in places far away from here, watching the Ozark Jubilee. My first memory of old time music is personal. I was just a little child when the Carter Family came to Butterfield, Missouri, my hometown. My Aunt Juanita said she found out they were just as poor as the rest of us when they stopped by her little store on their way out of town to buy food for the road because all they bought was cheese and crackers.

I was about six- or seven-years old when they played the Butterfield gym, which would've made it around 1951. All three of the girls were there: June, Helen and Anita, and their Aunt Sara and Mama Maybelle. I remember they'd built a big square box for a stage out there in the middle of the basketball court. The gym was packed full of people, more than I'd ever seen, and we were down at the end under the basketball goal. I couldn't see a thing because I was so little. So my dad put his hand on my back and kind of pushed me up between people so I was out in front and there they were: all dressed up in party dresses with wide skirts and ribbons on them and singing like angels.

Being a kid, I don't remember a single word to a single song. What I do remember is that as they were getting ready to begin one of their songs, Maybelle, who was playing guitar, tried to get more comfortable in her chair. She sort of hitched herself forward and as she did, the chair made kind of a rude noise on that hollow wooden box of a stage.

Well, it was the Carter Family. Nobody was going to laugh. But instead it got very quiet. And then June, who was already the family cut-up, leaned up into the microphone and said, "Mama just wanted you to know that was just that chair that scooted." And that brought the house down. We laughed til we cried. We may have liked them before, but we loved them after that.

The music they sang has held a special place for me ever since. It's probably one of the reasons I sing old-time music. Speaking of that, I'll be singing a June Carter song just a few weeks from now at the 14th annual Old Time Music and Ozarks Heritage Festival June 20 and 21 down here in West Plains.

I'll be singing along with a bunch of others including Big Smith and the Whites, those wonderful singers who played the Carters in the movie "O Brother Where Art Thou?" You remember them riding around in that pick-up truck singing. Well, they're riding down to West Plains next month... probably not in a pick-up truck.

Anyway, I wanted to be sure you knew about this and put it on your perpetual calendar because every year down here from Friday morning til Saturday night on the third weekend of June, we throw a party in celebration of the good old days. Old-time music, old-time foods and old-time handwork. We even have a mule jump and the Bob Holt National Jig Dance Competition. Then there's storytelling, basket making, woodcarving, turkey calling, ice cream making, old time square-dance making, quilting, gunsmithing, and a black powder rendezvous, where the

43

guys and gals who wear buckskin and shoot flintlock rifles and pistols create an encampment demonstrating life in times when such habits and gear were ordinary. And that's about as old time as it gets. Man, you name it and it's in there. It all amounts to a pretty good time. And it's all free except for the gas to get here.

JUNE: Audio Theatre Returns

Down here in Howell County we may think of ourselves as a quiet little backwater most of the time, but this month the dust had hardly settled from the Old Time Music Festival when the National Audio Theater Festival people returned to town. They're the people who work in radio and related fields. They do the sound for movies and television and the record industry and iPods. And all manner of other stuff.

I love it when they come to town because it's a great learning opportunity for me and the other folks who attend and a fine entertainment for everybody else. People come to study sound editing, voice acting and audio production, and to get a first look at the latest gadgets and technology. For me it's a valuable chance to improve my editing skills and not have to bother the folks at the studios so much by asking so many dumb questions.

This week I got to go out on a field-recording trip with Renee Pringle, who you may know from NPR's Morning Edition, to collect sounds for tonight's two-hour performance by the entire NATF Workshop that will air before a live studio audience.

They do this every year, and it's a real hoot – always an extremely entertaining event. But as usual, they need sound effects. One year they needed the sound of water drops falling way back in a cave. To get that you have to go way back in a cave. Renee loved that, but I managed to be elsewhere. Another year they brought in an Air Evac helicopter and recorded the sound of its landing and taking off. This year there was a story about an old lady who lived on a farm. Therefore they required the sounds of pigs, chickens, a rocking chair and a mule. So Tuesday morning we went out by Hodgson Mill on Bryant Creek to Colin and Leslie Collins' farm to see what we could get. We got a bunch of stuff (insert farm sounds).

I wish Renee's folks back at NPR could have seen her out there following around an aggravated bee with a microphone (bee sounds). Anyway, we were almost entirely successful. We got the chickens to cackle, the rooster to crow, the bee to buzz, the rocker to rock and the pigs to do quite a number of things. But as for the mule, well, sometimes you just have to improvise.

Back at Cup o' Joe's, we found someone who said they could bray like a donkey.
(man making donkey sounds)

He was good enough, or strange enough, that it set the town dogs to barking.

(dogs barking, more donkey sounds)

It was close enough for radio theater.

JULY: Somethin' Might be Gainin'

Summer is upon us. The farmers' markets are bursting at the seams with the fruits of the farmers' labors. But even this season of plenty seems a season of discontent, too, and it's not just the heat. High prices at the pump are making it harder to fill the pantry, and the news seems worse every day. Those of us old enough to remember talk of what it was like in the '30s wonder if we may be gearing up for another long run of bad times. I think about what Satchel Paige said: "Don't look back. Somethin' might be gainin' on yuh."

Now I know it doesn't pay to get too excited about the national news for a couple of reasons. Some of what happens out there doesn't get all the way here. My mother said that in the Great Depression nothing much changed except nobody had any money. But since they didn't have any money to begin with, they hardly noticed it.

The other thing is, the news isn't what it used to be. Time was, you could tell the difference between the supermarket tabloids with their three-headed Martian babies born to an Arkansas teenager and the more reputable sources that would just give you the facts. But by the time today's corporate media managers get through with the news, we don't know if what we're getting is what there is, or just what somebody thinks we ought to think.

Just the other day I saw an article in USA Today that talked about families who had adjusted well to the recent changes in the economy by growing a garden, raising chickens and substituting stews for their steaks, and peas for their pate. I thought that was charming. I might have tried that, except I was already doing stews and peas, and the dogs the townfolks left at my place when they couldn't afford to feed them anymore had already eaten my chickens. So those ideas didn't really help me much.

The next day there was an article in the Chicago Tribune about a group of African American people, led by their minister, who left the Chicago area in the 1960s and settled on a large farm near Cape Girardeau, Missouri. They took their children out of the city to raise them nearer to the life they had lived in rural Mississippi. They took them, as they said, back to the Promised Land.

Those children, now grown and with families of their own, described it as a paradise. But for them, it has become paradise lost. The children, having once known city life, took jobs off the farm instead of learning the skills of farm life. Where their parents and grandparents could grow corn and sorghum, raise pigs and chickens and cows, and feed the community on what they raised, the children could only make money. Now the land lies fallow, the children live in town and bicker over what to do with their lost heritage and dreams.

A sad tale, especially when placed against the blithe chatter about raising chickens and growing a garden as the quick and easy fix to our worsening economic woes. No mention is made of the months of effort and expense between the chicken and the egg, between the seed and the tomato. If we think gasoline is expensive, what might be the cost of a little good sense?

Those two stories called up a serious question in my mind. I know how to make do, and so do a lot of country people my age. But what about this generation now, who has no memory of hard times, or how to survive them.

I'm thinking it may be time we started making a bigger fuss over the gardeners, the librarians, the wisdom-keepers, those who remember how to do or find out things people may need to learn to do for themselves, things that, in hard times, help keep a civilization - civil. We might start by teaching that basic Ozarks rule, the one right after "take care of each other." It goes like this: Use it up, wear it out, make it do or do without. Maybe not as catchy as trading pate for peas, but more likely to get us through the hard times in these Ozarks Hills.

AUGUST: Running From the Race Business

Of all the things we talk about with the elections coming up this fall, what we seem to be talking least about, although it's on everyone's mind, is race. And I'm wondering if it's because there are so many of us who have very little room to talk.

Now I don't want to get into politics here. What's on my mind is history. I was talking the other day with a friend of mine who is of Japanese descent. She told me a story about her mother who grew up on a farm in Nebraska, of immigrant parents, She learned when she first went to school that she was different. The children played a game where they circled around, holding hands, and she was next to the teacher. She thought that was special until the teacher, instead of taking that little girl's hand, pinched up just the tiniest bit of skin so as to touch as little of her as possible. Her teacher did that. Isn't that something?

So when she could, she went to California, where she was a little less different, until World War II, of course, when she was rounded up and put into an internment camp, for fear she'd feel called on to become a spy for her native land of Nebraska?

Anyway, we can be stupid when it comes to race. So, I'd like to tell you another story, about my great grandmother, who we called Granny Luke.

She started out as Elizabeth Loveall, or that's what we always thought. Came here with her parents from over in the Carolinas somewhere and married and settled out on the western Missouri prairie in Newton County, at a little town called Gadfly. It's not there anymore.

The war came, and her husband took the union side. He met another soldier named Mark Gentry, and they became friends. He asked Mark that if anything happened to him, would he go tell his wife. Mark agreed.

Well, the worst happened. Mark went to tell Elizabeth, and some time later he married her. They had several children, among them, my grandfather. One of my grandfather's brothers had the curious name of Boudinot. Another brother, M.L., whom everyone called Boomer, had another curious habit of offering to fight anyone who suggested the family might have any Indian blood.

Well.

Years and generations passed, and Mark died. Elizabeth married Mr. Luke and became Granny Luke, and she and everyone in that story passed on into history. Then one day in a book I stumbled onto the name Boudinot again, and discovered it was the name given the son of John Ross, first chief of the Western Cherokee, who had led his people across the new United States on the shameful, sorrowful Trail of Tears. What was he doing among us?

So I went to learn more about Elizabeth. There were no Lovealls on the Cherokee rolls. But when I looked at census records to see where she had come from, her parents appeared to have come from three different places, in three different years, and there was no record of them having settled here. They apparently came to Missouri, dropped off their daughter and disappeared. Later I found other records from before the 'a' was added, and their name was Lovell, a fine Cherokee name.

Well.

So it appears I may be an Indian, at least partly so. Not quite white, some would say. Sorry, Uncle Boomer, but I really don't mind that. It's a rich history, and I'm in good company. I don't know many in these hills who could say much different. Some are proud of it and some not. I almost couldn't prove it, because those Lovells were so good at hiding their traces to protect Elizabeth. I don't know if it's too late to get my name on the rolls. It's certainly too late for me to apply for scholarship funds, although a tribal newsletter might be nice.

Even without official proof, I'm sure of her identity and mine, from two things. One, I have a picture of her, with her black, straight hair, high cheekbones, eyes as deep as the ages. Two, I have another story, passed down from Uncle Boud from his first day of school when the other little kids came out and danced around him in a circle, pointed their fingers at him and chanted, "Your maw's a squaw, your maw's a squaw." And that brings me to the children and how they always seem to learn less from what we teach than from how we behave. If we're honest about how we've been doing, surely to god, we can do better than that. It'd be hard enough to answer for if the race category had just one box, marked "human."

Author's Note:

The September, 2008 episode was based entirely on an interview from which the original recording can no longer be recreated – another that fell victim to my lack of technical expertise. It was an entertaining (I thought) little audio jaunt over to a fledgling vinyard in Oregon County where I admired the grapes, picked some and sampled a vintage. It deserves a return visit. Watch for it in the next volume.

OCTOBER: A Good Old Ghost Story

This isn't the story I intended to tell. I had prepared a perfectly good rant about the economy when I suddenly realized my program would air on Halloween. And who could resist the chance to tell a good old Ozarks ghost story for Halloween.

I know you hear this sometimes from people who are about to tell you a big fat lie, but this story is the gospel truth. And as you know, a story you swear to by the gospel has to have at least some truth to it. First of all, the house I grew up in, the former town hotel, happened to be haunted, not by anything horrible but just by regular folks, I think. It was hard to be sure because they were invisible. And they didn't do anything to scare us really except for that one time. They'd just do things like turn on my bedroom light when I got in late from a ball game or gather in the north room and talk in worried whispers if anybody in the family was ill. And sometimes they'd try to let us know they were there – mainly by coming in the front door and walking down the hall to the kitchen, noisily. It was an auditory phenomenon mostly. We rarely saw anyone, but there was this one time they let their presence be known in no uncertain terms.

It all started when we took our neighbors over to Seneca, just on the MIssouri side of the Kansas state line, to see the spook light. It was the middle of winter and quite cold when Jack Stanphill, the Butterfield school principal, came in the post office and mentioned that someone had told him some nonsense about a spook light. My mother, the postmaster, was surprised.

"You've never seen it?" she asked.

He hadn't, and he was surprised she took it seriously. Well nothing would do but we had to take him and Thelma over to see for themselves. We went; we saw it. Jack was amazed and considerably sobered by the phenomenon. He finally worked out in his head that it had to be reflections from some car lights coming from over west, maybe the Oklahoma Turnpike.

"So, would it have been wagon lights when people saw it back in the 1800's?" my dad asked him.

Jack was quiet the rest of the way home, and we figured we'd scared him. So when we got back to Butterfield, we invited them in for a cup of cocoa to warm them up before we sent them home. And as we sat with our cocoa the talk worked its way into other unexplainable things. It was a short leap from there to ghost stories, and we told a bunch of them.

After a while they left and we went to bed. I was just about asleep when the front doorbell rang. I thought Jack and Thelma must have forgotten something, but when I got to the door there was no one there. I went back to bed and my head had just hit the pillow when, "ding-dong," the doorbell said. I sighed and got up to look again and, again, nobody was there.

My dad called down the stairs, "Marideth, see who's at the door."

"Nobody's there," I said.

"Check the back door," he answered.

When I went, nobody was there either, and the bell rang again. I heard my father grumbling as he came down the stairs in his jammies. Before he got to the bottom, the bell rang again. "Oh," he said, "I know what's happening.

Marguerite, come down and see this." The bell was now ringing every minute or so.

Now my dad was an electrician who had installed that bell himself, so he knew how it worked. He explained it to us as we stood there in the cold. The bell button was attached to a plunger that pushed a metal piece up against another metal piece to connect the circuit and cause the bell to ring. The button and plunger were plastic and they weren't attached to the metal piece. The bell was shorting out because it was old and the cold had caused the two metal pieces to get too close to one another. "Come outside," he said, "and I'll show you." Outside, he pointed to the button. "See," he said, "the bell will ring but the button won't move."

Well, it moved, and the bell rang, and we looked at each other and back at the bell, and at that point it begins ringing non stop, "Ding-dong! ding-dong! ding-dong! ding-dong!" In fact it rang until he took the bell apart.

The next morning he put the bell back together, and it worked just fine, and it never rang by itself again. But then, we never told ghost stories at the hotel again either.

Happy haunting from These Ozarks Hills.

NOVEMBER: Ordinary Miracles

Another Thanksgiving has come and gone. When you get as old as me, there are a lot of them to remember and a lot to be thankful for. That's what I've been doing, while recovering from too much food, too many desserts, and a lingering cold.

Last year at this time, I was telling you about a trip I had just taken to southern Arkansas to have Thanksgiving dinner with a dying friend. Three months later she was gone, so I'm especially grateful that I had that time with her.

I will always remember that Thanksgiving after my parents died in '66. I was 23 and lost when my dear Aunt Maude, who was also spending the holiday alone, insisted that I drive her down to the AQ Chicken House Restaurant in Springdale, Arkansas, so she could buy me a turkey dinner. And all the way there and back, she told me stories of my mother and father and how they met and courted, stories I'd never heard before. Now she's gone, too, but I will never forget her kindness and her insight. She told me what I most needed to hear.

Another Thanksgiving that stands out is the one I spent in Costa Rica some years back. Thanksgiving, which is not a holiday in Costa Rica, had kinda sneaked up on me. I went looking for a place that served something like a traditional Thanksgiving meal and ended up at an outdoor café owned by a homesick American. But I came late and got an apology because all the turkey dinners were gone. Resigned, I ordered from the regular menu. But when the food came to the table, there was the turkey dinner, complete with cranberry sauce. The owner shared with me the dinner he'd made for his family, saying, "I always make too much." I still give thanks for his kindness toward a stranger from home.

It's good to be thankful, even in hard times, to stop and reflect and remember the good things in our lives.

Here's one. I'm thankful for the election and that it's finally over, along with the noise of the campaign ads, news analysis and the grousing over all the irritating things in human character that we get so riled about. Some of us are satisfied at the outcome, some not. But here's the thing that for me seems the most beautiful and awe-inspiring about the whole process. We had an election. The candidates fought and argued, and we argued with each other and probably said a thing or two we regret – or not.

But at the end of it, when the votes were counted and the winner named, when some went out dancing in the streets and others turned off their televisions and mumbled prayers, we all got up the next day and went back to what we were doing before all the fuss started. We didn't go on killing sprees. We didn't bomb city hall. We just went back to work. You only have to look out at the rest of the world to know what a miracle we have experienced. Despite all our individual and shared flaws, our prejudices, our foolishness and pettiness, and every kind of wrongheadedness -- the process worked. Churchill said that democracy is the worst system in the world, except for all the others. He was right, and we proved it again.

So before we get through with giving thanks, we might want to add a big one for the rare gift of living in a country where such things can happen regularly and so reliably as to seem ordinary. So thanks for ordinary miracles. Thanks for the gathering together of families of all sorts, and warm hearts – and the kindness of strangers.

DECEMBER: There is No Peace Without Peace

Here in the dark of Midwinter, we have come once again to the heart of our traditions. Whether they be Christmas or Hannukah, Kwanza, Ramadan or Solstice, something in the season has called us together, tribe by tribe, in celebration, of our kinship. And in nearly every tradition, this is the time of the year that we speak of peace. Peace on earth, we say, in all the languages of earth. Friede auf Erden. La Paz, Shalom. Or Assalaamu Alaikum in Arabic.

I had the great fortune recently to spend some time with Jim Scott, who you may remember as the guitarist in the Paul Winter Consort. He is also a singer and a Unitarian Universalist minister, and has become sort of a modern-day circuit rider, going from concert to concert and congregation to congregation, talking about spiritual peace. These are the words of one of his songs from his performance in concert at the Yellow House Community Arts Center in West Plains:

When despair for the world grows in me
and I wake in the night at the least sound
in fear of what my life and my children's lives may be,
I go and lie down where the wood drake
rests in his beauty on the water,
and the great heron feeds.
I come into the peace of wild things
who do not tax their lives with forethought
of grief. I come into the presence of still water.
And I feel above me the day-blind stars
waiting for their light. For a time

I rest in the grace of the world, and am free.

We talked about peace after his performance.

Jim: "There is no peace without justice. We've said that for years. People all say that, and I guess I believe that. But where are you gonna get your justice? Through fighting a revolution or through violence? Maybe it's just gonna be through forgiveness and generosity, and you come to peace through grace. I mean, somewhere the cycle of violence has to stop, and someone has to say 'That's it.'"

"That's a good point," I said. "I mean, what is Christianity based on but peace, through turning the other cheek?"

Jim: "Sometimes you just have to forgive, and accept that the way that peace is gonna come is through peace. I learned that from Martin Luther King, so I get it that there is no peace without justice. I think there is no peace without peace, and that's what that song is about, 'I am peace and I am waiting.' That's what I was trying to say."

Words to ponder. It seems that like war, if we want peace, somebody has to start it. Let peace begin with me. And there's the bugaboo. If you're like me, finding peace in your heart takes some serious looking. We're often too busy just trying to get by. Some days, we'd just as soon fight. There is the Ozarks joke about the fellow who came down with Irish Alzheimers. Seems he forgot everything but his enemies. Honestly, there seems to be no end of things we can find to fight over down in these hills.

We've even cooked up a war about Christmas. That all started when somebody noticed that Christmas is just one of the midwinter holidays, and so the greeting was changed to Happy Holidays, It's the inclusive form of Merry Christmas.

But to those who see the world as just Christmas, and Other, that meant war. Does this mean that I must refuse your good wishes because you didn't say them right? Or that I should wish my Jewish neighbors a merry Christmas instead of happy Hanukkah? Or if I don't know their cultural heritage, should I just assume they're Christians, or they ought to be, and they should assume I'm right, not just ignorant?

Some would have it so. I would say to them, "If you want to protect Christmas, stop fighting about it." Jim Scott is right. Peace is the way. It's a hard option. It means giving up our best fantasies, the ones in which we're always the hero, armed to the teeth, here to save the day. It's not the day that needs saving. It's that pretend hero in us who believes we're doing good while behaving badly, who believes torture can make someone tell us the truth. But if someone tortured us, wouldn't we tell them whatever they wanted to hear?

Terrorist and freedom fighter, it all means the same, you know, depending on which side of the fence you're talking from. How can we hear one another except by listening. Do we need to add a Department of Peace to the Presidential cabinet?

Peace on earth. Worth not fighting for. Worth the world, in this and every season. Peace. Pass it on.

2009

JANUARY: By Any Name, It's Time For a Party

Now I have to tell you, these cold, dismal, icy winter days are beginning to get to me, and I have a theory about why that is. Before you get all wound up, reminding me that we're in a recession, and we're ALL depressed, I'd like to point out that this time of year in any year gets depressing, and most cultures have learned to adapt. They throw a party. They may call it a feast day, but it's really a party.

What do we do? We send somebody out to see if Puxatawney Phil saw his shadow. And we hope he didn't. The good news would be that on Groundhog day, nothing happened. Is that dopey, or what?

I've been checking it out. Everybody else from way back has a holiday they can celebrate about now. The Irish call it Imbolc, which means 'In Milk' for the arrival of the new lambs. The druids called it IMmulg; the early Germans called it Disting; the Stregans called it Lupercus. The Catholics called it Candlemas, or in Mexico, Candelaria. It's the festival of the lights, or the Feast of the Virgin. The Romans celebrated Venus, the Greeks Diana. They dedicated the whole month of February to the Goddess Februus, the Goddess of Fresh Starts. Now if ever there was an excuse to throw a party, wouldn't that be it?

In checking out this phenomenon, I was most intrigued by an account of the festivities in Bulgaria, where, as most students of history know, a recession has been in progress since before most of the citizens were born.

Their feast day, held while we're out looking for Phil, is called Tryphon Zarezan, for Tryphonos, the vine trimmer.

65

Saint Tryphon, according to numerous Bulgarian sources, is worshipped as the guardian of vineyards, and this festival is in his honor. It is observed not only by vine-growers, but also by market-gardeners and tavern-keepers, or so some versions of the story go.

Early on a particular morning the mistress of the house bakes some bread and cooks a hen, which - according to tradition - is stuffed with groats or ground corn and homemade sauerkraut. The hen is roasted in a shallow copper pan. Then a loaf of bread, the hen and a buk-litza full of wine are put in a new woolen bag. With the bags over their shoulders the men go out to the vineyards, make the sign of the cross, and make three ceremonial cuts, a ritualized trimming. They anoint the vines with wine, after which they load a well-to-do villager whom they've chosen as "King of the Vineyards," onto a cart.

The king is crowned with a wreath of vines, and a garland is placed across his shoulders. Then the vine-growers, pull the cart to the village, accompanied by bagpipes and drums. When they get there, they stop at each house for more wine. Everyone has a drink, and anything left is thrown on the king, while everyone shouts wishes for a bountiful harvest. The king finally says amen or its equivalent and they adjourn to his house , where they feast for two days, and perform a ritual known as 'trifuntsi' which gives everyone protection from wolves. Women avoid scissors, in order to prevent the wolves' mouths from opening. They do not knit or sew, but make another ritual bread. After serving it to their neighbors, they put morsels of it in the fodder they give to the animals - thus protecting everyone from wolves.

On the next day, the story goes, it is good to serve some lighter food to those who ate and drank too much the day before, to make them feel better and clear up their minds. Now that's what I call a party.

All the traditions in our melting pot culture, and we have to venerate the eyesight of a groundhog? Now who thought that up? I'll just bet it was the Puritans. And where is Puxatawney, anyway?

What would be the harm if we were to declare instead an annual cheer-the-heck-up day? We could trim up a few fox grapes, bake some good bread and adjourn to my house out on the farm. I'll make the chicken. And we can drink to a brighter day, whether Phil shows up or not.

FEBRUARY: Hard Times and More Coming

Hard times, and more coming. That's what we're hearing. But that message runs counter to what we in the Ozarks know, especially at this time of year when any sensible person is looking at seed catalogs, ice storm debris and the yard that didn't get mowed last fall. This time of year, our usual lament comes when we realize that all those plans for a long winter's nap are probably not gonna happen.

Out here in my neck of the woods there's plenty to think about without obsessing over a possible Depression.

After all, it's almost time for spring to, well, spring. The crocuses know it, popping up everywhere, bursting with promise and good cheer. The other day I completely forgot where I was in the seasons, muttering over the last bit of grim economic news, and almost bit the head off a cheery little bloom. I actually told it to get serious, before I came to my senses.

I remember a wise thing I heard once from a woman who said, "How would the world be if we just listened to ourselves? We know all these things, but we don't listen when we say them. For instance," she said, and picked up a container of a popular soft drink from which she'd been sipping.

"We describe the act of wising up by saying we've come to our senses. Now, if I actually, literally, came to my senses, would I be putting this stuff into my system? No. But we get distracted by the struggle to live in this world."

I understood what she meant, and I think most people would. There is, after all, that famous Ozarks phrase describing a person in poverty, "He was so poor he couldn't even pay attention."

But we also know, deep down, that feast and famine both have their seasons. It's up to us to know when to change course, batten down the hatches and get ready for whatever's coming. I'd say we're there, wouldn't you?

But while the Lords of power and money are moving assets offshore and finding ways to make failure look good, we in the Ozarks have a simpler solution. We grow a garden. And if things look really bad, we grow a bigger one. Even if we're not going hungry, somebody's gonna be.

That was my family's solution to the last Depression. It worked for them.

So do you have a garden? Do you want one? It's time to decide. I know that because the robins have come back. They're early. I saw one just the other day, looking disgusted, standing on a melting ice floe in the middle of the birdbath. "Times are tough all over," I told him.

And yes, I talk to robins. And the peepers who are also popping out early. Just last week they were out croaking their amorous little peeps in the farm pond. And I went out and yelled back, "It's February, you dopes!" That shut them up for all of two seconds before they were back at it again. What can you do? Spring is trying to spring. Life wants to live, after all. And that's the message the hills are sending this week. All this obsessing is depressing. It's almost time to plant potatoes, and the early peas could go in now, if you want to take a chance on them. Go on. Get your hands dirty.

A garden is good for you. Do you know where your garden is? Mine is moving, now that I've recaptured a piece of pasture by moving a fence. I've drawn the plan out so many times I've actually missed several of the gloomy news forecasts. I feel like gardener Ruth Stout, when asked why she didn't take the newspaper.

"Surely if something dreadful happens, someone will come and tell me," she said, and went back to planting her peas.

I'm not suggesting we stick our heads in the sand and pay no attention to the serious matters facing the nation today. But neither should we dwell on the things we cannot change and let go the things we can.

Head in the clouds and hands in the dirt can give the heart balance. I mean a garden can feed you, often better than anything you can buy anywhere else. It can be good exercise, a chance to commune with nature or a relaxing meditation. But most of all, it can restore your faith, something that can be sorely needed in difficult times like these, when many of the institutions and people we've depended on have turned out to be unstable and untrustworthy. My mantra is one I borrowed from that gardener, Ruth Stout, who said, "When you plant a bean, it comes up a bean every time. It never, ever comes up a tomato." In the Ozarks Hills it will soon be time to plant beans – and tomatoes.

Author's Note:

MARCH This month's segment was done by a
guest host while I was recovering from surgery.

APRIL: Homes for Potatoes

In April, my radio broadcast on KSMU in Springfield, Missouri, took a different twist. I couldn't get to the studio, so journalist Missy interviewed me by phone.

"Marideth do you want to tell us where you are and how you got there?" she asked.

"I'm at St. John's Hospital up on the fifth floor, but I'd rather be anywhere," I responded.

"I don't blame you because we're having some nice spring weather," she said.

"That's what I hear. I came in the first time more than a month ago and had surgery for uterine cancer. They got it all, and I was recuperating. So I decided to go ahead and have my garden plowed. I had a spot picked out; the only thing in it was a big tree stump. When the tractor came in to plow, there were roots everywhere. The fella couldn't get enough steam to go fast enough to turn over the dirt. It was just a mess. I couldn't plant it the way it was, and I was trying to find someone with a tiller. Then I woke up one morning with a high fever and discovered I had an abscess from the surgery. I've been in the hospital ever since.

Shelton: "I'm so sorry to hear that, but it sounds like you are in good spirits and ready to get back to your garden."

Sisco: "Yes, I am. And actually other people have gotten back to my garden for me. This was the year I planned to plant a big patch of potatoes. I had a lot of fun varieties. I ended up with 30 pounds of potatoes, no garden and me in the hospital! So my friends have been rushing around, calling people they know who have gardens asking, 'Have you got a row?' 'Have you got half a row?' I have no idea where my potatoes are, but they're all over town."

Shelton: "So your friends have taken it upon themselves to find homes for your potatoes?"

Sisco: "Find homes for my potatoes, that's right."

Shelton: "What a great community story."

Sisco: "It is. It's a great community down there. West Plains is my adopted home. I came back to the Ozarks from California and went back to my old hometown, and it wasn't the same anymore. I went over to West Plains and found the Ozarks I left behind. The people are just so kind and generous. When they called me and said they were finding homes for my potatoes, I just about cried. You can ask people to take you to the doctor or bring you groceries but it's a reach to ask people to plant your potatoes."

Shelton: "It makes me feel good to hear your friends and neighbors are stepping up in that way. When you head back to West Plains, you'll have a good reason to sit down with those friends to share a good meal. Maybe with potatoes?"

Sisco: That's right. Absolutely with potatoes.

MAY: Decoration Day

Earlier this week, I made the long drive over to what used to be home to pay my respects to those who've gone on before. In my case, it was to Mount Pleasant Cemetery near Butterfield, Missouri.

Memorial Day has always been problematic for me... maybe because I never heard it called anything but Decoration Day until I was grown. And by the time I was grown, I'd already made several trips to that cemetery on other somber occasions that had other names. I lost both my parents when I was in my early twenties. By that time, I'd already lost both grandfathers, my Great Aunt Laura who rocked me to sleep and my Great Uncle Tom who taught me how to sing.

So I had decided I'd had enough of cemeteries and I didn't get the whole decorating thing. I didn't see what there was to celebrate. For a long time, I had nothing to do with the cemetery at Mount Pleasant, and I persuaded myself it had nothing to do with me.

Well, sometimes a person gets wiser and sometimes they just get older. If they're lucky, they finally learn that the resentment of being abandoned by those you love, if you let it, can turn into gratitude for all the love and knowledge they left behind to sustain you. I didn't let it. Not for a long time.

Then in 1988, a tornado touched down in Butterfield and did tremendous damage, including one death. When I heard the news, my thoughts went racing back over the miles and time and, for a moment, I was overcome with concern for all the people I knew there. Then I realized every single one of those I worried over had been safe for years. They were up on the hill at Mount Pleasant, out of harm's way. Things began to turn around for me then, although it took a few more years and a few more funerals before I finally got comfortable with re-visiting all those ghosts and the memories they brought with them. It took one more death, that one not in the family, for me to finally grow up and claim all those memories as my own.

When my mother was a child, she had become fast friends with a little redheaded girl up the road named Johynee; they spelled it different, so you'd know it wasn't a boy's name. She and Johynee stayed friends all through their growing-up years, sharing adventures and confidences, my mother's of becoming a novelist and Johynee's of traveling the world. They vowed that at the end of their adventures, they would meet back in Butterfield and grow old together. Well, my mother married this handsome boy who joined the Navy at the start of World War II. She spent those years waiting for him to come home from traveling the world, while her stories went untold.

Johynee joined the Army Nursing Corps and was sent to London, where she worked at an Army hospital all through the Blitz and never got to go anywhere. When the war was over, she took a job in California, got married and had five kids. She and my mother wrote letters back and forth but hardly saw each other at all.

They were reunited, finally, in the most poignant of circumstances, after my father died and my mother came back to California with me to renew some of those old friendships. But she was ill and didn't know the cause, and Johynee, who was the head nurse at the hospital by now, took her in for an exam. It was left to Johynee to tell her, and me, that she was dying. That was more than 40 years ago.

Much later, when her children were grown and her husband had passed, Johynee came back to Butterfield to stay. And when I went to visit her, shortly before she died, she told me that for all those years, whenever she came home to visit, she had come to Mt. Pleasant and left a single yellow rose, the symbol of joy and friendship, on my mother's grave. She explained it by saying simply, "I loved her. You have to honor that. It's all there is."

So I have taken a lesson from Johynee. I'm new at the custom of decorating graves. But now when I go to Mt. Pleasant to visit those I loved, I bring roses, pink ones, for love and gratitude. There is one for my mother, one each for all the others, and one for Johynee, who showed me how to come home.

JUNE: The Tomatoes of Human Kindness

Ever since I first went in the hospital back in March, I have been telling people that I had a bad spring. Some folks thought I said I had a bad sprain, so I've had to explain that my ankles are fine, and so is the rest of me, mostly. But after my bout with cancer, followed by a nasty abdominal abscess, fine is maybe bragging a bit.

I'm still a little weak, suffering, according to my doctor, from deconditioning, from those weeks in the hospital. So no arm-wrestling or triathlons for me just yet. Still, going in for surgery just two days after the vernal equinox and still in physical therapy when the solstice arrived, I pretty well missed the springtime altogether. For a gardener, that's hard.

I already whined in public about needing help to plant my potatoes. Then, between the plant-a-row-for-the-hungry folks and those inspired by the flagging economy to plant a garden for the first time – I finally got to the nurseries to discover the plants were mostly picked over or gone, and almost no one had seeds. So this gardener has done a fair amount of muttering, grousing and saying unkind words over the potato patch, the collection of large pots and the straw bales that comprise this year's very late garden.

Eventually I had to fess up to the fact that it was not unkindness that got me to this place. Au Contraire. It was the essence of kindness that I found at every turn in this difficult and extraordinary journey. Kindness that found people willing to find room for some of my potatoes in their gardens. Kindness that brought a neighbor to till the potato patch at the farm so I could plant the rest. The kindness of a

77

friend who drove me to the hospital and sat with me in the ER while the fever and pain were translated into a diagnosis. And the never-failing kindness of all the nurses, doctors and aides who offered care and encouragement as I made the long and arduous journey back to health.

And it went on. There were friends and strangers who donated time and other resources to make my days at home, still on IV antibiotics, less of a struggle, and one who cooked a freezer full of meals for me, just because she wanted to help.

I owe thanks to so many people that I don't even know where to start. So many went out of their way for me, not because I deserve it or have earned it in any way but simply from the kindness of their hearts. It is a debt I can never repay, although I've thought long and hard about how that might be done.

One thing I can do is to make sure their kindness bears fruit. I can put away my petty complaints and tend my garden with thanks, taking in the peace that it offers. I can recognize the sanctity of my Mother Earth on whose belly I have once again begun to thrive.

I can start my days by giving thanks for friends and for the grace and goodness of strangers who offered up their skills to bring me back to health. It doesn't seem like much in exchange for having my life back.

So maybe I need to look a little harder at kindness and try to remember that it is a practice, not a condition. It acts to open the heart for the practitioner as well as the receiver. It takes no special tools. It's just one of the things that makes us sentient beings, along with a bundle of other traits that it seems we're always having to clean up after.

Kindness, too, leaves its mark on the world. I remember Ruth Stout, another gardener who once said that she had more faith in plants than in people because when you plant a tomato, a tomato is what you get, Not a bean. Kindness, too, when planted in the heart, bears reliable fruit. This spring, I've discovered that my garden is far bigger than I thought. And the fruits it has offered up have healed far more than my body.

I wonder if Ruth knows about the tomatoes of human kindness. I suspect she's grown a few. Providence willing, before the summer is out I'll have plenty to share.

JULY: Safe in the Middle

Last week, a friend of mine asked if I could fill in for a fellow who had been in an accident. He was to be the moderator at a panel discussion on health-care reform. My first question was. "Why Me?" Of course, given my recent experience with hospitalization, I thought maybe that was why they wanted me. But no.

Instead, my friend said they wanted someone who could be neutral.

Neutral? I thought. I'm the most opinionated person I know. I thought about what she said all day, but I concluded that most of my opinions are, well, moderate.

I've never seen the sense in going way out in left field or the other direction either, just to be the way-outest of the way out. In fact, I'm usually the first to start looking for a compromise when people around me are at odds. Without a way to find common ground, arguments can turn into grudges and grudges into feuds. Before you know it, someone has done or said something that someone else finds unforgivable. Then it's war. Near and far, we've certainly seen that happen often enough to recognize it.

I had that whole phenomenon explained to me once by a Native American friend down south, a Shawnee man who startled me when he expressed this notion.

"Just about all the troubles of the world can be traced back to men not letting the women be in charge," he said.

I asked him to explain, thinking maybe I misunderstood.

"Men only think in straight lines, while women think in circles," he said. "Women think about before and after, and

80

yesterday and tomorrow, and the old people and the babies and what they need and what you have to be prepared for and how to get everybody fed. They can look all the way around a situation," He shook his head.

"Men don't do that. They are like little children all their lives. They poke the guy in front of them and kick the guy in back. They're so wrapped up in ego and one-upmanship that they'll sooner or later end up in a fight that leads to murder and war. Then the world just goes to hell."

I had to admit, when I thought about it , that he was making a lot of sense. If a person can only think in straight lines, when they get crossways with one another, there's no way to fix it unless someone can help them see it another way.

He also said, "Men know how to do all kinds of things, but they don't know what to do. If there's not a woman there to help them work out what to do, then it's all one-upmanship and war. "

I thought about that all day too.

Well, the panel did fine, and probably would have done just as well without me. Moderator I was, but no moderation was needed. Everyone was cordial, answered all the questions intelligently, and were civil to each other, even when they had to agree to disagree.

But right in the middle of things, when I had nothing to do and was bouncing things around in my head over this notion of "moderator," I remembered a conversation I'd had years back with a colleague who quizzed me about my politics. I had just come from covering a meeting where the proponents of the left side and the right side had almost come to blows because the other side just wouldn't see it their way. I was disgusted with the whole pack of 'em.

Have you ever noticed that when you put together the people who are the most vocal and rabid representatives of

81

the farthest left and farthest right, you can't hardly tell them apart? They're alike enough to be kinfolks, each one trying to prove who can throw the biggest fit. Right then I announced my political preference in no uncertain terms. "I'm a rabid moderate," I said.

Well, I have to admit I haven't changed as I've gotten older. I'm still focused on the middle path. And I've discovered something along the way. If you can manage to stay exactly on the white line in the middle, you can avoid most of the traffic.

Author's Note:

The following segment was not broadcast on public radio due to its political content, which is not an issue here.

AUGUST: The Politics of Health

A few nights ago I had dinner with some friends whom I don't get to see often enough. All of us were over 65, and we didn't talk long before we got to the subject of health challenges. Bob talked about the bone disease that had put him on disability.

Allison told of the cancer last year that had taken so long to diagnose and left her so helpless for awhile.

I groused about my surgery and the infection that followed, and how long it took to get back on my feet.

Where could we possibly go from there but to a discussion of Medicare? And from there into other areas of health care and what we thought most begged for change.

We laughed about how discussions of living wills have descended into threats of death panels, and how some sensible people seem bent on saving not their options or their bank accounts, but only the insurance company's profits. It's a strange world out there, we agreed.

But what struck me most at the end of the evening was what a thoroughly civil conversation we'd had. One of us was a lifelong Republican until recently, one a Democrat of the historic yellow-dog variety and me, the rabid moderate.

We not only talked to one another. We listened. We didn't always see everything the same, but we heard one another. It was an excellent evening.

It made me wonder just how we've come to this awful incivility on the part of some participants at the recent town hall meetings on healthcare reform.

It's an important subject, and ought to be talked about. I don't see how anyone thinks a point can be made by making so much noise that no one can be heard or bringing along an assault weapons.

I mean, when was the last time you brought a gun to a conversation? Or threw a tantrum when someone said something with which you disagreed? If the point of the healthcare forums is to discuss what people want to do about health care, some folks are missing the point. Or they think their brutish behavior is the only point worth making. It's worse than not being polite. It's not civilized.

I don't know about you, but I take some little pride in the notion that, after several thousand years swimming in war, pestilence and testosterone soup, many nations of the world are beginning to become more aware, more able to to raise themselves up into complex, working civilizations.

Until now, we have been one of them. But the shrieking mobs shutting down the debate at the town hall meetings resemble the antics of enraged chimpanzees beating their chests and itching for combat. How is that related in any way to civil discourse?

It isn't. Anyone who's been through elementary school can recognize a schoolyard bully. If you're really upset at the proposed healthcare changes, why not use the forum's opportunity to explain your position? Tell why it's better, instead of shutting down the democratic process by drowning out everyone else. This disruption of discourse benefits no one except, perhaps, those major corporations that want nothing to interfere with the status quo.

I may not understand everything about this reform business, but I know someone is making a killing off a health care system that doesn't have my health at the top of its list. I suspect if we took all the money being spent on trying to stop this conversation, we could all pay our premiums.

Well, I could go on, but here's what I really wanted to say. The world is changing, for better or worse. And very few of us are so conservative that we believe nothing should ever happen for the first time. Conversation about controversial issues is necessary. Those who try to stop it have no one's best interests at heart. Let me suggest an alternative approach.

Be nice. Be fair. Be civil. Stick to real facts that can be documented instead of bringing out the boogeyman. Don't make up stuff. Show respect for other views and try to understand where they're coming from. Either leave your guns at home or understand you will be seen, but you will not be heard. Everyone will assume you intend to shoot something. And above all, act like a grownup. The kids are watching, and you are teaching them far more than you mean to.

SEPTEMBER: A Heavenly Ozarks Autumn

The seasons have turned a corner this week. We've had to say goodbye to another summer, at least according to the calendar. The autumnal equinox is just past. I always have trouble adjusting to that because here in the Ozarks the weather sometimes remains balmy well into October – or not.

Even though the equinox signals a balance between daylight and dark, it doesn't seem balanced. The weather here is always full of surprises, a fact that's easy to forget when you're entranced by the beauty of the season. It's a reminder to get ready for that sudden shift: A blast of wind straight out of the north or a sneakily quiet, star-filled night when the bottom drops out of the thermometer. We awake not just with cold feet but with the sickening realization that the houseplants – grandma's begonias and all – are still out there on the porch, uncovered.

Then there's the wild harvest that you're liable to miss altogether if you live in town. The black walnuts are pretty widespread. But blessed indeed are those who have a source for hickory nuts, pecans or persimmons. Or fox grapes or hazelnuts or the almost nonexistent chinquapins.

The wild Ozarks is truly bountiful just now. It leads me to considering what my particular harvest amounts to. I had hoped to be able to provide a potato report for you this month. The ones I lamented about last spring seem to have done really well. Trouble is, I got them in so late they're not finished growing. I've been out in the patch practically every day tapping a toe, waiting for a sign they're ready to come out.

Part of my impatience is because I want to plant my garlic there, and I'd like to get it in and settled before really cold weather. But there's another motive, I must confess. I wanted to tell you about how many pounds of potatoes I got from the seed potatoes I grew and the ones planted by friends.

That was last spring, just before I discovered I needed surgery. Through a combination of miscalculation and blind-sidedness, I ended up with 30 pounds of seed potatoes that I couldn't plant. I couldn't even get the garden tilled. Friends were shaking their heads over the predicament I'd gotten myself into. So this fall I thought a little boasting about a splendid yield might be fun, at least for me. But the 'taters won't be hurried, and I've had to stop and reflect a little. What I've come to is this. I could tell you that with the help of some kind friends, I planted X pounds and got back Y pounds in return. And someday I may do that.

But there are other things that flourished in the spring and summer of my debility. Because some friends brought straw bales and rabbit manure to my home; helped me move heavy bags of planting mix; carried away some of the potatoes and raised them for me; tilled my garden and helped me fill containers, I have already reaped a bounty of friendship, not to mention the tomatoes, chard, peppers, green beans, eggplant and way too many cucumbers to know what to do with.

My daily mantra had to change. I'd been saying, "Just get me through this day." But when I looked out on my little garden I had to say, "I am blessed beyond measure." You can't measure that by the pound.

So like any gardener, I'm going for the practical approach. I'm making pickles. Bread and butter pickles with a little curry added. Since there's no way to say thank you enough times to enough people, I'm gonna let the pickles be sweet for me. It'll take a lot of pickles. I told the cucumbers that. They responded with a bushel of hefty green blimps. So I'm all set. Just chunk them up, salt them down, add some ice, steep overnight and throw in a pot with sugar, vinegar and spices.

And then let the scent carry me back over the years to when I stood on tiptoe watching my aunts and my grandmother do the same. It's all good, this Ozarks life. And it's the best time of year. A time for pumpkins and persimmons and hazelnuts and all the rest of the wild harvest. And for us, too, to reap what we have sown, either with our own hands or the hands of the ones we love.

OCTOBER: The Tick-Tack Trick

Halloween is here again, that special night when children of many ages dress in mad outfits and fall upon their neighbors demanding candy. They all know the phrase "trick or treat," but few know what that means anymore. It's simply a phrase to make polite the demand for candy.

In the Ozarks, though, where memory runs deep along with some arcane traditions, the message remains clear: It means "give me a treat or else." Those who smirk and say, "Or else what?" have lived in town too long or they're not from here. They've not awakened on November first to find their windows covered in soap or paraffin or their mailbox upside down or a wagon on the roof of the barn…or a car…or a tractor.

In the Ozarks, just about everyone knows the phrase really means treat or else trickery. On Halloween, nothing is safe. Nothing is sacred. One old man in my hometown got so weary of having his outhouse turned over every Halloween that he vowed to shoot the next person who tried it. And on that fateful evening, he settled down to wait in ambush inside the outhouse, shotgun in hand.

But the tricksters got wind of his plot and simply waited until they could hear him start to snore. They sneaked up behind the outhouse and turned it over on its door. The man, besides nearly being shaken to bits in the crash, had to shoot his way out. That story still remains in the fabric of my town's humor after many a year.

In West Plains, people still talk about the night an unnamed collection of boys disassembled a Ford Model T and reassembled it on the roof of the opera house. So it goes. The tradition of trickery remains alive all across these Ozarks hills.

So on this occasion, I thought it might be fun to share a bit of old-fashioned trickery, one that's not been heard of much outside folklore circles for a very long time. I was reminded of it when the basic technique, without trickery, was demonstrated at the recent annual Ozarks Studies Symposium at Missouri State University - West Plains.

The idea is to take a piece of stout cotton twine, tie a knot in one end and thread the other end through a hole in the bottom of a tin can. Have a friend hold the other end of the string while you hold the tin can and stretch the string tight. Then rub a cube of violin rosin up and down the string. The string becomes just like any other instrument string while the tin can acts as the amplifier or sound box. If done right, the can emits a piteous, non-musical howl that's truly blood-curdling. It's called tick-tacking. It's quite loud and if it's coming from behind a tree on a dark, Halloween night, it can truly scare the bejesus out of a person.

But that's not the trick. Here's the trick. In daylight, go to the house of an unsuspecting neighbor or family member, being sure you haven't picked one who has a weak heart or otherwise delicate constitution. On the outside walls of the house, search until you find a nail that has worked its way loose enough that the nail head sticks out about an eighth of an inch or more but is still firmly attached. Tie tightly to the nail the end of a long piece of string, long enough that the person holding the other end of string can remain out of sight.

Go on about your business until nightfall and then return to the house, violin rosin in hand. Locate the other end of the string, stretch it tightly and begin to rub the rosin up and down the string. With luck, the entire house will become the sound box, and those hearing it may think the house is coming apart. At the very least, they may be convinced that they've acquired a new ghost.

At this point, the perpetrator will face an ethical dilemma: Do you tell the people in the house about the trick and trust that everyone will have a good laugh over it? Or do you keep still and hope they never catch on to the trick or the trickster?

One thing's for sure. If you like these folks, you might want to confess before the "for-sale" sign goes up in their yard. Good neighbors are important in the Ozarks, and no matter how good the joke, they'll need to know when it's over.

NOVEMBER: Giving Thanks for the Now

Another Thanksgiving is behind us, and as always, I wonder how long this remembering to give thanks will last. Sometimes for me, the feeling is short-lived as I get into other things. Something irritates me, and I wander off into resentments and ironies and sarcasm, all of which have their place, but not necessarily a good one.

Someone told me once that in some cultures, every word in the language that refers to gratitude also implies some resentment, as though to say, "Oh, sure, now you've done something for me, so now I have to be grateful." Not exactly a positive attitude. And then I read the other day that too much positive thinking is ruining the country. I couldn't quite get my head around that one. It led me to think about this holiday that is specifically for the purpose of celebrating thanksgiving and of being grateful for our good fortune. Even as I say that, I'm already hearing some grumbling out there. What good fortune? We're in a recession and at war, and we've been robbed by the banks, and on and on. Certainly we are no stranger to hard times.

But then I think about my young friend who recently completed 30 radiation treatments for a brain tumor and does not yet know the outcome. And yet she forges on, reading, writing, rejoicing in new opportunities and new knowledge. She is busily at work participating in the National Novel Writing Month, or NaNoWriMo, where the goal is to try to write 50,000 words in a month, brain tumor, and homework, be damned.

This remarkable display of the courage to keep forging on, not denying, but merely disregarding the challenges and the naysayers, is enough to shame me for my little worries and resentments. I think of other friends who have survived things such as cancer, and who make of every day a chance to celebrate life joyfully, disregarding the shadow that lurks just out of sight. It takes courage to give thanks with no strings attached.

I know some will say it's their faith in God that keeps them going, just as others remind us that the fates are merciless and do not heed our call. And I know that none of these who forge on despite circumstance are doing it out of a lack of fear.

Some define courage as Grace under Pressure. It may be that, but it's also something else.

I remember confessing once to a friend that I wished I had the courage to take the next step toward something I desired in my life, but I was afraid. The wise friend replied, "It's not courage if you're not afraid. Courage is when you're afraid, but you do it anyway."

Well. There went my out. So I took the step. It was hard, but everything worked out eventually. And I ended up in a far better place than if I had succumbed to my lack of faith in myself.

So where's the lesson in this? Who are we thanking and for what?

Whether we call on the great undefinable by one of the 9,000 names of God, or the great mystery, or the source of all things, we probably should acknowledge first that there are thanks to be given, just for the great good fortune of being alive on this green earth at this precious moment. Or as that great Zen-Episcopal scholar Alan Watts put it, for Being Here Now. Having survived 66 years of life, and cancer, and heart surgery, and California, I believe I can safely say that that's enough for me, just being here now. And when I throw in friends who know me well and like me anyway, and I can look out the window every day on these Ozarks hills, I am the owner of blessings untold.

If there's one thing I would change, it would be the hurt we cause each other, either on a global scale or a very personal one. Life is hard enough without trying to ease our pain by passing it on. I'm hoping that with Thanksgiving fresh in our minds, we can find a gift that is more precious than anything we can find in the shops. The gift would include the courage to disregard the things that we fear in life and instead offer gratitude for all that is good in this great journey of now after now after now. Don't give resentment a seat on that bus, because it's bad company.

DECEMBER: A Larger Family

'Tis the season again for holiday celebrations, whether Christmas, Hanukkah, Kwanza or Solstice. The longest night of the year is upon us, when the earth ceases its northern tilt and heads sunward again. If you're near Stonehenge, or its little cousin the engineering students built up at Rolla, Missouri, you can stand in the circle and see the sun rise in the notch reserved just for solstices. Certainly the merchandisers are happy. People are buying presents like they did a decade ago. And certainly, we all are looking for better times.

But I think I caught myself saying Merry Christmas once too often, while leaving the home of a family whose elderly mother is just out of intensive care, the outcome still uncertain. It reminded me that for many folks in many places, the holiday season is often not all that merry. There are families with people serving overseas in grim situations, or in hospitals or gone. People estranged from their loved ones by conflict or illness or distance. Or older folks who've seen friends die, families dwindle and days of silence where laughter used to be.

This stirred up a memory of one of my darkest Christmases, the year my parents died. I was 23, out on my own, I thought. But then found out what that really meant. I had roots in a tiny Ozarks town where my mother was postmaster, like her mother and father before her. We had aunts, uncles and cousins galore. I didn't even have to put an address on letters headed home. Just Postmaster, Butterfield, Missouri.

Then with hardly time to catch my breath, I was orphaned. I had no home address. I spent Thanksgiving with an aunt who, like me, was still in Butterfield, but like me was alone for the holiday. We drove down into Arkansas to the AQ Chicken House for dinner. We talked long, told stories, laughed, and had a good time.

But by Christmas, I was lost. I didn't know what to do, how to continue or where I belonged. I couldn't just go back to what had been before. It was gone. And I couldn't bear the loss. I was a picture without a frame, a boat left adrift, a castaway.

On Christmas Eve, with a heavy heart, watching the snow blowing into drifts down the country lanes and more in the forecast, I remembered an invitation from an old friend in Springfield to come share Christmas, and I went. It was seventy miles up snow-covered highways in driving wind and cold, creeping around curves, the defrosters not quite keeping up with the icing windshield wipers. It was exhilarating. I learned that night that adrenaline, carefully applied, can be a very handy, if temporary, first aid for a broken heart.

My friend and fellow musician, Rodger, lived with his mother, Pauline, in a tiny, two room, two-story house behind the old Sorosis House on Walnut Street. Today the old Sorosis house is the student exhibition center at MSU. Pauline, a gifted and prolific artist, suffered from severe rheumatoid arthritis. Her mother, who helped care for her, lived next door at the Sorosis women's club.

That night, when I crept into the snow-covered parking lot between the two buildings, I found a path to the larger house had already been cleared for me by other vehicles. Pauline's brothers, Justin and Nelson Keifer, had arrived with their families from their homes in Kansas and Oklahoma, and the house was lit with many lights. Music and laughter greeted me as I knocked, followed by warm hugs and merry greetings when I stepped through the door. Dinner was on the stove, and Justin was about to unveil his latest creation. He was a beer-maker, and he was proudly handing out bottles of his newest batch of home-brew for us to sample. The bottles were handsome brown longnecks with impressively printed labels, titles displayed in elegant gothic script. I took one, inhaled the aroma, then burst out laughing when I deciphered the name: It was "Keifer's Rottensox"

It was splendid, especially when combined with good food and good friends, some of them brand new. I have no recollections from the rest of that night. But the next day more friends and family arrived. We ate, we sang songs, and I left late in the afternoon on thawing roads, whistling a tune and feeling oddly that I had come back to earth from some faraway, dark land. I understood then that there is always a larger family. If they remember you, or even if they don't, sometimes when you least expect it and you need it most, they'll take you in.

After forty-some years I still remember that Christmas, driving home in the afternoon sun with a full belly, a full heart, and a special gift of Christmas cheer, a six-pack of Keifer's Rottensox.

My Christmas wish is that we all remember we are part of a larger family and do our part to make sure no one is left out in the cold.

2010

Author's Note:

The "Winter's Bone at Sundance" piece that appears next is decidedly out of character for this series of essays in general. It is included for the sake of as complete a record as possible, and because it does refer tangentially to the Ozarks, as the film Winter's Bone was filmed here. However, it's mostly about me and the Sundance experience. If you're happy with the way the series is reading so far, please feel free to skip the next segment and spare yourselves the experience of me blabbing on about the movie and the Park City experience.

JANUARY: Winning at Sundance

In this segment of the radio series "These Ozarks Hills," KSMU's Missy Shelton talks with Marideth Sisco about the trip she made this month to Park City, Utah for the Sundance Film Festival. Much of the film "Winter's Bone" was shot in the Ozarks and Marideth's singing voice is featured throughout the movie. "Winter's Bone" won the two top awards at Sundance. Missy Shelton talks with Marideth Sisco about the movie and her experiences at the festival.

Shelton: "Joining me on the phone from West Plains is Marideth Sisco. Marideth is just getting settled back here in the Ozarks after a trip to Park City, Utah, for the Sundance Film Festival. She's in a film called "Winter's Bone," which took the top prize at Sundance. Marideth, can I say we're glad to have you back in the Ozarks?"

Sisco: "I'm sure glad to be back. It was an experience out there but 40,000 people in a town the size of Park City is just too many folks."

Shelton: "I'm sure. And let me say congratulations on "Winter's Bone" earning two prizes at Sundance this year, including Best Drama and the prize for screenwriting."

Sisco: "Thank you. We were just tickled to death. When people really like a movie, you get your hopes up and you think that you've got a good chance. Those two awards come at the end of the show, so we applauded for everybody else.

And then it came up to the screenwriter's prize and that went to 'Winter's Bone.' And that was the first prize that they gave us and we thought, 'Oh well. That's it. That's the one.' So, we settled back in our seats and prepared to congratulate somebody else. But when the woman on stage began to talk about the mythic journey of the hero, we looked at each other and said, 'That's us! That's gotta be us.' Then she said, 'Winter's Bone.' I told somebody later that I always thought I knew what an adrenaline rush was but I was mistaken. I found out what it really is on that Saturday night."

Shelton: "I should mention that 'Winter's Bone' only secured a distributor during Sundance so most people in the Ozarks have not seen the movie. But you had a chance to see it while you were in Utah. What did you think?"

Sisco: "It was beyond my wildest hopes. It was hard for me, even though I knew how good they were. And I knew they had won awards before. But it was hard for me to get around the idea that a bunch of people from New York could come down here with their crew and make an authentic film about the Ozarks. But by golly, they did it.

"Missy, they took such care along the way. This is something I only found out about in conversations with them over the last week. They even went to people's houses in the neighborhood there where they were filming and started conversations. The actors would go in and listen to people talk so they could get the accent right. The costumer actually went into people's clothes closets to look at what they wore and would find things like a really worn Carhardt jacket. They'd trade them a new jacket for that jacket because they wanted that jacket in the film. It's so authentic, so real. It's a slice of the really backwoods Ozarks. I hate to say backwoods because it sounds so primitive, but the culture there is like the culture was 150 years ago. It hasn't changed all that much. They may drive bigger cars but they're about the same people. To capture that and do it with such respect, I thought it was an elegant film. I really did."

Shelton: "Marideth, I wish we had more time. Again, congratulations. I'd like to ask you to close out our segment today by singing the version of the Missouri Waltz that actually opens the movie. I know it's you singing and would love to hear that as we close out here today.

Sisco sings:
"Hush-a-bye my baby. Go to sleep on Mama's knee.
Journey back to these old hills in dreams again with me.
It seems like your Mama was there once again.
And the old folks were strumming that same old refrain.

Way down in Missouri where I learned this lullaby,
when the stars were blinking
and the moon was shining high.
And I hear Mama calling as in days long ago,
singing 'Hush-a-bye.'"

FEBRUARY: The Essential Artist

I had intended to say something about spring, but I understand it's been cancelled, at least for the present. There's nothing like frozen water pipes and a malfunctioning hot-water heater to let you know just where you stand in Nature's estimation. In any case, life has intervened, and the subject of spring and winter's passing has had to step aside in order to honor other passings.

The older you get, you know, the more of your traveling companions in this life's journey seem to have reached their destinations. So it was with two of my favorite people this past week. One of them you probably know if you live in Springfield or its surrounds, if you've encountered his work.

Robert E. Smith was Special with a Capital S. Stories about Robert and his doings are so widespread that I couldn't put them all into this little essay. Most people understood that Robert was differently-abled, but few could decide where to put him on the divide between developmentally challenged and mad genius. He may have been a little of both, but I always leaned toward the latter.

Of all the stories about him, one that was my favorite happened in the early 1980s. Robert, for the few people out there who never encountered him, was a prodigious producer of paintings that documented life in the Ozarks. He often painted events such as elections and holidays with great attention to detail and full of fantastic characters and circumstances as well. Well, Robert had been considering his own circumstances as an artist and had begun to doubt his talent. He thought maybe folks were complimenting his work just to be nice. In fact, he began signing his work Bob Smittyboob.

Then someone suggested he get in touch with a bona fide art professional and have his work critiqued. The details are sketchy, but he apparently went to see Missouri State University art professor Jerry Hatch with some samples of his work, and Hatch told him his work was wonderful, very honest, yet so surreal. As Robert was leaving the art building someone asked him how the critique went, and Robert replied, "He really liked it. He said it was sure real." And so it was.

The other artist we've recently lost was less well known and more certifiably mad, but there was no question of her genius as a fiber artist, writer and musician. She obviously knew the extent of her tenuous ties with reality because she renamed herself; the name she chose was Kiteweather. In her saner moments, she prowled area thrift stores from here to St. Louis, searching for cotton knits in colors she could use for her stunningly crocheted rugs and blankets. Sometimes she wrote clever tales about the people in her life, or in the culture's spotlight. She spun songs full of wit and sorrow and at times would roam the Ozarks Hills, sometimes silent, sometimes crying and calling, always fiercely elsewhere.

When she knew she was dying, she sent people away so that she could pay attention to the process. She didn't want to miss anything. For many years, in Don McLean's words, she had suffered for her sanity. But as time passed, she seemed less driven by madness, and more fully engaged in her art. For my 60th birthday, she sent me a blanket that featured a fire to warm my feet, forests and rivers to feed me, a blazing white sun to light my way and the aurora borealis to color my dreams. I felt blessed beyond measure by this artistic embrace. I sleep under it every night.

It is often said of such iconic figures in our life's landscapes that their likes will not come again. I'm not convinced that's true. They were singular figures. In fact, you could say that after they were made, those molds were broken. And yet that special blend of art and madness is bound to come again. We need it. The days of our own lives are enriched by its presence. Edgar Degas, one of the best of the Impressionists, once said "Art is not what you see. It's what you make others see." It was here that I saw their true genius. Each, by their art, carried a message, a swift poke at our common reality that said, "Really? You think so? Well, watch this."

If the value of our lives consists of what good we accomplish, then what better can we do than to face the life that's given us, to embrace chaos and make of it art. We need the artists, every last one. We need someone to model fearlessness for us.

Author's Note:

Again, the following essay was deemed beyond the mission of public radio due to its political content, so it appears here for the first time. If you distain political discourse, please move on to the April segment.

MARCH: Whither Socialism

Like many of you, I've been watching the ongoing contentiousness over healthcare reform. Rabid moderate that I am, I've been trying to steer a middle course through the arguments. In particular, I've tryed to avoid the debate over whether the changes amount to a leap toward socialism.

At my age, I've gotten suspicious of labels, especially those that may be just a stand-in to represent the boogeyman. But I was curious to understand what people meant by socialism.

So I went to the dictionary and looked up the word. In fact, I consulted several dictionaries to see if I could get a clear consensus. It took awhile.

I finally decided to go with Webster's definition, although there turned out to be four of them. I rejected the last one outright because it was all tangled up in Lenin and Marx, and I was pretty sure they're not in this fight.

The first entry defined socialism as "Any of various economic and political theories advocating collective or governmental ownership and administration of the means of production and distribution of goods." Hmmm. Well, I know the government has become a pretty large stockholder lately in some of the big banks. But hospitals and insurance companies? Factories? Not so much.

Then I considered definition two: "A system of society or group living in which there is no private property." We're talking commune here, right? I'm pretty sure that if there were anything in the healthcare bill about communes we'd have heard more about it by now.

At this point I was left with definition three: "A system or condition of society in which the means of production are owned and controlled by the state."

I still couldn't get any of this to fit. So I looked at the arguments again, using the middle ground to try to figure out the real dispute. And I found the missing word.

Regulation. That's what this argument is really about. One side believes that the unregulated healthcare industry is out of control and harmful to the public good. The other believes that any regulation of private industry is a step toward state control of all industry, which would be harmful to the public good. We're in a situation where each side is defending the public good as it sees it. Intentions, on both sides, are for the most part honorable. But then someone starts tossing around the word socialism, as if it's the devil's spawn. Everybody bristles up for a fight and loses sight of the real argument.

Where, in all this, is the public good? And I've got to tell you honestly, from my little spot in the middle of the road, that something as large as the public good is just too vast for me to get my brain around. And I'm no judge of vast societal trends that might tell us whether one bill passed by Congress would turn us into a socialist state.

I have to come back to the idea of regulation, and here, I'm stuck with my own personal bias, fueled right now by a malfunctioning water heater. The regulator's gone bad, and a week of cold showers has put me in a foul temper. One side of me wants to take a hammer to the thing; the other side just wants it to work. I'm a walking, shivering embodiment of the whole healthcare debate.

In my search for the middle ground and some warm comfort, I suddenly remember a remark from a woman in the suffrage movement. I don't remember who, nor can I reproduce the exact quote. It addressed the curious nature of our culture in those times. The gist of it was that a woman must rely on one man to protect her from all others, except in those instances where she must rely on all others to protect her from the one. It's the same dilemma as those who would defend the public good. I don't envy them their work, as I'm still stuck in the middle, waiting for hot water while trying to stay out of it.

APRIL: Spring Tonic

This has been the most beautiful spring. There's a remarkably silly Ozarks saying in regard to the season, that goes:

Spring has sprung,
The grass has riz,
I wonder where the flowers
…is.

Yes, the weather has been splendid. It's a good thing, too, because time is at a premium. So many things to do and never time enough to accomplish them. I'm up to my ears in garden seeds and too few places to plant them; too many places to be, most of them at the same time; well, you know how it is. After this last week, I was so tired out that I got to wondering about the general state of my constitution. After all, I'm in my late 60s, and although I'm not worn out yet, I'm definitely worn. The last time someone asked me how I was, I told them I'm in pretty good shape for the shape I'm in.

But the truth is, I get tired, and it's aggravating. Tired is for winter, when a person can hole up and get some serious reading done. But spring is for, well, springing, like springing into action. Instead, I find myself reciting that old poem that my grandmother used to quote, with the line that goes, "My get up and go has got up and gone."

Well, that's not going to fix anything. So I went out yesterday and wandered around the yard, trying to work up some enthusiasm. I did get a little excited for a minute, seeing all the shoots of pokeweed starting to pop up everywhere. Surely you've noticed. Maybe you've already cooked up a mess.

I like mine simmered in two waters, with a dash of vinegar and maybe a dab of butter or bacon fat. It's one of the necessary rites of spring. A tonic, if you will. Hmm, I thought. Maybe that would shake me out of my slough of despond. It was when I was trudging back to the house to get a colander and a paring knife that it hit me. Poke wasn't what I needed. What I needed was some sassafras. You want to talk tonics, sassafras is nothing short of an Ozarks miracle drug. Now it's not good for everything. It's no use at all on a snakebite. But for everything from a case of the doldrums to easing a heavy heart, it's just the ticket.

Now I know about that bunch of researchers who fed a mouse about a gallon of sassafras tea once and decided from his reaction that it was probably poison. But who's gonna drink a gallon of anything? Tonics are taken small and measured by the dram. It's a ritual we could do in our sleep, if we're old enough to remember it.

Here's what you do. Go out and find a young sassafras sapling in an unsprayed fence row. You'll know it. It's the one with the leaves that look like mittens. Poke around in the soil underneath it until you find some good-size roots, as thick as a pencil or bigger. You'll know them, too; they're bright orange. With a hoe or a mattock, chop out about a foot-long section or two. Take it in and scrub it well until all the dirt and little root hairs are gone. Chop about a four-inch section of it in little pieces and put it in a cup. Peel the rest and put the root and peelings away in a saucer, in a dark place, to dry. Pour boiling water into the cup, let it steep for a few minutes and sweeten with sugar or honey.

Now stop. Admire the warm, delicate color of the roots and the tea they have made, just for you. Breathe in the scent. Isn't it elegant, so wild and mysterious. Have a sip. When you heard grandma talking about spring tonics, you didn't picture this, did you?

111

Now sit back for a little while and think about all the beauty and mystery of the natural Ozarks, a place where lives this wonderful gift of the earth. Feel yourself sink into your own place in things. Then finish the cup before it cools. See? It's a beautiful day in the Ozarks, isn't it?

Ok, break's over. Get busy. Spring has sprung, the grass has riz, and it's time to mow it.

MAY: The Unsung Ozarks Summer

Summer is here again, and I can't say I'm too pleased about it. Summer in the Ozarks is beautiful, but it's my least favorite season. There are the bugs, the heat and the humidity. I can hear someone saying right about now that "It's not the heat. It's the humidity." Well, I don't know about how it is where you are, but on this side of the Ozarks it is, *too*, the heat. *And* the humidity. These days, songs like "Keep on the Sunny Side" and "In the Good Old Summertime" are not on my song list.

Truth be known, I seldom perform the old standard pop songs, even though I grew up with them. It's because of what my parents did to them. They sang every time we got into the car, which, since my father traveled from job to job, we did quite often. Wherever we went, they sang all the way there. And I learned many a song from them, sitting there in the back seat, wondering where we were going next.

I've kept the habit of singing for all these years and am apt to burst into song at the drop of a hat. But not those songs, not the ones learned from my folks. That's because I know better. My parents spent years deliberately perfecting the wrong words to all the songs and sayings they could think of. That's right. They traded the real words for their own. Even when they heard a comic song and learned it, they improved upon it until it satisfied them.

To this day, I can tell you the number of days in a month by reciting that old favorite rhyme:

Thirty Days Hacienda. April, June and No Wonder.

113

All the rest have 31 except Grandma,
and she drives a Ford.

You see what I mean? Then there's that old song from an old musical, you remember the one, called "Yes, We Have No Bananas." I recently learned the real words and found to no surprise that my parents had made alterations in that as well.

The chorus line of both versions goes
--Yes, we have no bananas, We have no bananas today.

So far, so good. But if you were to sing the original verse, it would go like this:

We have string beans, and onions
and squashes and scallions and
All kinds of fruits and Hey!
Yes, we have no bananas, and so on.

But my parents' words went like this:
We-e-e just killed a pony, so try our baloney,
it's flavored with oats and hay, hey,
Yes, we have no Banana yeah,well …

I was fully grown before I realized that I had diligently memorized the wrong words to a score of songs. And since I had been collecting songs to sing for years, I didn't always remember which had been altered and which had not.

My parents died when I was in my early 20s, and over the decades I gradually weeded out the altered versions of songs until I didn't sing them anymore. But they're still there in my head. I can only think of one they didn't alter, because it was already so silly, and tended to alter itself when sung. The written lyrics are as follows:

"Mares eat oats and does eat oats,

and little lambs eat ivy.
A kid'll eat ivy too. Wouldn't you?"

But when sung, they turn into this:

"Maresy Dotes, and Dosey Dotes
and Liddalamms eedivey.
A kiddle eedivey too, wouldn't you"

They loved that song so much that for a time they called
me Maresy.

The song I'd nominate as being perfect for summers such
as this is a lovely but horribly sappy old ditty called "In the
Shade of the Old Apple Tree."
Wouldn't you know it, there is also a comic version
called, "In the Crust of the Old Apple Pie."

Well, my folks were delighted by the comic version but
couldn't tear themselves away from the fruit tree version. So
they hybridized, and came up with a version I like.

Their version goes like this:

"In the shade of the old apple tree, there is something for
you and for me
It might be a pin that the cook just dropped in, or it
might be a dear little flea
It might be an old rusty nail.
Or a piece of a puppy dog's tail
But whatever it be, it's for you and for me,
In the shade of the old apple tree

Author's Note:

Here, in the following entry, is another of those "outtake" segments where I've left the Ozarks and am on the movie trail. Again, the movie is about the Ozarks. But the segment is all about the movie opening in Lttle Rock and the Big Apple. If you're into continuity, feel free to skip it. It's a distraction.

JUNE: The Whole New York World

This is Marideth Sisco for These Ozarks Hills. Most years, I really don't like summer all that much because I have to spend my time indoors under the fan instead of outdoors in the garden. But I'm seeing it differently this time because I've just come back from a very busy week in New York City and a week before that in Little Rock, promoting the movie "Winter's Bone."

If you haven't heard of this film by now you must be out of the country. It was made in the Ozarks; it is about a part of the Ozarks; and the book on which it is based was written by Ozarks native Daniel Woodrell.

It was a very good book and now it's a very good movie, if I do say so myself. I was in it. I was the old lady singing in the picking session and other places. So this past month I was out plugging the film, first in Arkansas and then at the New York openings.

Speaking of New York City, even though I was filled with preconceived notions, it was a pure delight. It caused me to change my somewhat snooty thinking about the essential inferiority of urban life.

New York City is its own world. The food at its worst was terrific and was sometimes too good for words. The accommodations down in lower Manhattan were cozy and offered a view of an old part of the city that was once a thriving garment district. Most of the roofs still had their old water tanks on stilts, from which they still draw their gravity-fed water.

And right among them in that homey skyline view, stood the Empire State Building. I have to admit I was charmed.

The traffic was crazy, but I figured out what you do about it. You don't drive. You hire someone else, an expert who can perform an elegant high-speed slide between delivery trucks and pedestrians and get you to your destination, untouched and on time. They're magicians but they're called cabdrivers.

As you can tell, I had a very good time there. I expect I'll go back.

I'll return to Little Rock as well. I didn't get to see nearly enough of the Clinton Library, and I didn't spend enough time at the River Market down the street from my hotel. The hotel, though, even with its marble columns and all the trappings of southern culture, turned out to be just a little rich for my blood.

Now I should make clear that the accommodations were great. They were paid for by the festival, and I am definitely not complaining. The large room was outfitted with a comfortable bed as well as a couch, coffee table, dining table, desk, large TV and two maids a day. One maid called in the morning with two newspapers and advice on where to go for breakfast. She tidied up the room and made the bed. The other brought smiles and delicious sweets and turned the bed down in the evening. I gotta say that both of them had accents and manners way more like mine than anybody I met at breakfast.

The film festival itself was well-organized and great fun. They took wonderful care of me, and I'd say that even if we hadn't won the "Golden Rock" for best film. More unusual than the bronze trophy that came with the award was an item in the gift basket sent to the hotel by the festival management.

It was a talking action-figure doll with its own stand and certificate of authenticity from an outfit called "Toy Presidents." Yes, it was Mr. Bill himself in suit and tie and a button under his lapel. When pressed, the button activated a tinny, very eery comment once uttered by the president himself.

It is just such as this, apparently, that show business is made of.

I got back from Little Rock just in time to do laundry, repack and run through the shower, then it was off to the Big Apple for the New York openings. There, I answered questions at the Metropolitan Museum of Art, then spent an evening in a series of taxis, running between uptown and downtown to answer more questions about the film and the Ozarks. My favorite was when someone, referring to the people portrayed in the film, asked, "What do you call those people?" And I was able to answer, "I call them neighbors."

Two weeks well spent, and I'd do it again for this movie in which I played such a small part and feel such great pride. But there was nothing that could beat landing again on Ozarks soil, and making my way home out of the Branson hills and across the southern tier of counties down to my little farm below Hutton Valley.

All that runnin' around was fun and maybe worthwhile, but it sure is good to be home, even in summer.

JULY: The Heat

I don't know about you, but I've just had about enough of this heat. It doesn't affect me like it does some people, but it's plenty bad enough.

Legend has it that the Indians told the first settlers that they came here every year because of the beautiful spring and for the nut harvest in the fall. They were only passing through, though, they said, because nobody would be crazy enough to live here through the summer.

Well, you know that saying about the addled and the English out in the noonday sun. That's us. I meet my neighbors out going to Wendy's and Wal-Mart any time of day, in any temperature.

It's crazy. And it makes some people crazy. With the advent of air conditioning, such long-used phrases such as "He went crazy from the heat," have more or less gone out of fashion. But I'm old enough to remember when it was an every-summer thing to hear of someone keeling over while out at the wrong time of day.

I can remember 1954, when the summer got so hot I often came in exhausted from play in the shade of our silver maples to find my mother on the secluded back porch, ironing, in her underwear. I might add that she was not a woman given to such excesses.

I remember another odd occurrence during that summer at home, when my father's father came to visit. Years previously, this man had offended my mother so thoroughly over something that he had done to my father that she had said he would never be a guest in her house again.

"Well, but that was a long time ago," my grandfather said. "For heaven's sake, woman, it's hot out here." He tried to push past her and into the house. And when she attempted to shut the door against him, he wedged his boot in the door. Then he laughed at her.

Well, he must not have known the Gentrys, or he would have known that was a bad idea. Either it was the heat or the laugh, but she decided it hadn't been long enough for her. She reached down, all of her 5'1" self, grabbed the hammer behind the door for protection because my dad worked nights, and brought it squarely down on the toe of my grandfather's cowboy boot.

So he reconsidered and found a place in the shade to park his car. When my dad got home from the store, they went to the cafe and had a nice visit. We didn't see much of my grandfather after that.

That was one hot summer, all right. If I recall correctly, that was also the summer when we moved from Springfield to Washington State. I was just 11 years old, but I retain many clear memories of that trip. There were two large packing crates that held all of our household goods, carted off by a truck to the train station to be shipped out west. Then the drive down to my aunt Maude's in Barry County, Missouri, where we left the car.

I'm not sure, but I suspect that Uncle Gus bought the car, providing our trip money. One of those brief flashes of memory was from that leg of the journey in our 1934 Ford, the one that came to be known as the Elliott Ness car for its running boards and front-opening "suicide" doors.

We had stopped for gas on the outskirts of Springfield next to the new Colonial Motel. A gas war was on, and we laughed at buying gas for 19 cents a gallon. Usually it was 24cents. My grandmother was riding in the front seat and she had opened the door to catch what little breeze there was with the thermometer at the gas station reading 104°. As the attendant finished pumping the gas and my mother paid him his $2 and change, my grandmother called out, "Is everybody in?" Then she shut the door on her foot. Crazy times, as I said. We must have laughed about that for a month.

We stayed a few days to visit, and then it was time to go to Washington to meet my father. He had gone out earlier on the bus and found a job on the Hanford Atomic Project near Richland. My Aunt Juanita and Uncle Leonard were out there too, along with my cousin, Martonne, and her new husband, Danny.

They had been writing us about Washington and what it was like. They told us there were forests of asparagus along the irrigation ditches, free for the picking. And they had picked gallons of Bing cherries and made a huge cobbler, and ate the whole thing. Curiously, though, they said, there were no good apples. All of them had been shipped east.

The day for departure came. Aunt Maude baked two loaves of bread and a big batch of oatmeal cookies, and she fried two chickens. She wrapped each piece of chicken in a slice of buttered bread and packed it in a box along with the cookies and a couple of jars of pickles and some cloth napkins.

Gus drove us to Joplin where we caught the 3 am train to Kansas City. The conductor said he didn't want to disturb sleeping passengers, so would we mind riding in the lounge. We wouldn't, and we spent the rest of that night in large, swiveling arm chairs, the lap of luxury of that time.

We changed trains in Kansas City and spent two days and a night crossing Nebraska, Wyoming and Idaho before arriving in Pendleton, Oregon. It was sunny, dry and 80 degrees. And everyone was complaining about the heat..

AUGUST: Dog Days

Every time the year turns around to August, no matter if the summer has been variable or just miserable, like the one we're in now, we say we're in the dog days of summer.

When I was a kid and I heard people say that, I looked down the street to see how many dogs were asleep in the shady dust under the pickup trucks outside Goldie's Cafe. By August, the number was usually in the double digits, unless they'd been rousted out by boys using up the last of their fireworks. Somehow, the thought of tossing a firecracker under a truck to see the dogs scatter was simply irresistible. We didn't get out much back then.

I was grown up and far away from here before I learned that the dog referred to in Dog Days was not under a truck. It was up in the stars in the constellation Canis Major, which is Latin for Big Dog. Sirius, the Dog star, is the brightest star in that constellation – the brightest in the whole sky, in fact.

But what does that have to do with the sultriest days of summer?

Well, it's complicated, but I'm going to try and connect the dots.

First, the most important star to us humans, in terms of its usefulness to us, is Polaris. It's hardly the brightest star, but it always points north. In fact, its other name is the North Star. We can count on it to find the right direction when traveling. But how do we locate Polaris? For that we have to go back in time. You see, all this stuff was worked out a long time ago, when the Romans were trying to connect the star dots to make a useable map of the heavens.

That's why we have all those Latin names for constellations. When they imagined they saw a big dog and little dog in a certain pattern of stars, they named them Canis Major and Canis Minor. When they saw a big bear and little bear in another pair of patterns, they named them Ursa Major and Ursa minor. Later, folks who couldn't find those bears renamed them. Now they're the Big and Little Dippers.

Polaris is found by drawing an imaginary line up through the two stars that are farthest away from the Big Dipper's handle. Keep going and there's little Polaris, glowing away. And where Polaris glows is true north. This works better than a compass, which only points at magnetic north. But that's another story.

You see, while astronometrs were working all that out, they also noticed that Sirius, the brightest star in Canis Major, disappeared behind the sun during August. And since it got extra hot about that time, they decided that the big star was adding its heat to that of the sun. They thought the combination of the two was ratcheting up the temperature.

Thus, the idea of the Dog Days actually refers back to that conjunction of Sirius and the sun during the hottest part of the year. I had no idea. I was almost set to believe it made sense, and I was delighted earlier this week when the temperature began to drop into its proper place for nighttime. We're coming to the end of the Dog Days, I thought. Then I called up my new friend Google and got a surprise.

You see, there's also this little cosmic gizmo called the precession of the equinoxes. Over time it throws things backward out there in the stars. Stellar bodies move around, and they're not always in step with one another. Actually our little wobbly planet moves around, too, and so Polaris won't always be our North Star. Sometime about 13,000 years from now, the North Star will be Vega. I think I can wait for that.

In the meantime, this precession business has snuck in and moved the Dog Days. This year they started on July third and ended August 11. They've been over for weeks, and it's just now beginning to cool down.

Well, so much for understanding summer. I'm no better at that than I am at understanding the constellations. I think I found Polaris last night, but I searched all over for the dots that make up Canis Major, and I swear, all I could see was a duck.

SEPTEMBER: Harvest Moon

Autumn is upon us with harvest festivals, corn mazes and pumpkins of all shapes and manner. It's my favorite time of year, and I was going to hold forth on that subject until a question last week took me off on a whole other track. Jennifer Moore, my home-town pal who's a staple at KSMU public radio in Springfield, Missouri, called to ask if I could wax a bit on the subject of the harvest moon, since the one coming up was supposed to be a Super harvest moon. Well, it certainly was, taking place over parts of two nights while the sky was the deepest of blues. It was a short jump from there to moonlight, to lights of all kinds and finally to our relationship to light in words and culture.

References to light are everywhere. Love light, spook light, light in the forest, at the end of a tunnel, or in dark places, my life or on the subject.

We write songs about it: "Moonlight Sonata," "Moon over Miami," "Moon River," "Moonlight in Vermont" and, of course, "Shine On Harvest Moon."

This brings us right back to that harvest moon. Most of you already know that all the moons have names related to when they appear and in what season. After harvest comes the hunter's moon, the beaver moon, the snow moon and so on.

The harvest moon was crucial for the farmer who worked late in the fields and did the chores, especially in the days before we had headlights on the tractors. Or tractors. Hunter's moon was for getting meat in for the winter, even if you had to stalk an elusive prey into the night. Beaver moon was the time when the little dam builders harvested the last of the branches and twigs they would feast on in their lodges through the winter.

There's another reason we pay attention to the light, especially at this time of year. We are going into the long darkness. Whether on daylight time or standard, we are losing daylight at a rate of two minutes a day. Think what that must have been like in the days before electricity, before petroleum fuel, before dependable light was at our fingertips. We even rearrange the clock today to give us more daylight in summer and in winter.

Now I'm going to drag science into the conversation, just to mention something theorized almost a century ago, but proved only recently. Don't misunderstand. I'm not going to turn into a scientist after all these years as an itinerant musician and English teacher. I can't explain anything Einstein did. I can only marvel at Einstein's understanding that time can change and move slower or faster in relation to distance, but light cannot.It is true. Other scientists proved it.. So light is the only constant. Light, it seems, is universal, while the nature of matter, and time, are transitory. Imagine that. A universe built of light, with all the rest of it, and us, just the furniture.

I can't imagine it, or I couldn't, except for one thing, the theory at its simplest: It's all relative. I can imagine that, having been to Rockbridge Mill in full summer on a moonless night. The mill, with its attendant restaurant, cabins and trout hatchery, is off a narrow, winding road in the heart of Ozark County. You almost can't get there from here, but that night I did. After dinner I wandered out to the mill to sit at the edge of an enclosed loft with an open side above the millpond and dam.

Soft lights glimmered from the serving area of the bar, but the night outside was as thick as velvet. I stepped over to the railing and looked out at the steep hillside opposite.

Suddenly, the hillside was alight with candles that flickered, went out and reappeared, thousands of them. They were fireflies in unbelievable numbers. Just for an instant, I had the sense that these were tiny sparks of life, looking back at the little spark that was me. It was the same change in perspective one gets when watching fireworks or a meteor shower. Things shift, and you are no longer lying down on the earth looking up but suspended in space, the earth at your back, looking out at the vast light show that is the cosmos.

The moon, whichever one is up there, is closer, more intimate, and keeps us in a familiar perspective. I suppose that's good for everyday situations.

But once in a while we need to be reminded that there is more to life than dependable things. Sometimes we need to be taken out, shaken off and reminded of who we are -- little sparks of life itself, thin, essential filaments in the fabric of a universe of light.

OCTOBER: An Ozarks Autumn

Here we are again at All Hallows Eve. Preparations are underway to go bump in the night, or go wailing on the moors, or go hilariously door-to-door dressed in the outrageous or macabre. Soon, with luck, we'll again be assailed by hordes of ghosts and goblins, most of them your neighbor's kids out to do a little innocent banditry. These days, the most we older folks have to be concerned about is parceling out way too much candy. That's just fine. Treats we can do.

In older days, trickery was much more likely than treating. Though it was sometimes funny and often perplexing, by now we've probably enjoyed all we can stand of soaped or waxed windows, overturned outhouses and odd farm implements on top of the barn. But there's more to the season worth mentioning than ghastly goblins and tipped-over toilets.

Just now, the Ozarks is dressed up in the best of its autumn finery for a last fling before the cold and dark of winter arrives.

Everywhere on my little farm there are views large and small that snatch the breath away and interrupt my earnest feet on their morning walk. For the observant, there is a feast for more than the eyes, as the wild harvest makes its last effort to bring us through the winter unworried about hunger and lack. The trees, in addition to dazzling the eyes, have been raining fruits, from walnuts, pecans and hickory nuts to persimmons and the last of the pawpaws. For the squirrels,

129

there are buckeyes and horse chestnuts of every size and description. It is bounty worth celebrating.

Granted, if you're a harvest gardener, the joy of the first tomato is long gone and the persistence of okra and peppers is prompting a longing for one good, hard freeze to put an end to them so they can be appreciated as a reminiscence, rather than as the tag end of a too hot, too long summer. Funny, isn't it, how we enjoy remembering the fruits of our labor long after the memory of the work it took to gather them is past.

But this has surely been a harvest to remember. Apples and peaches, although small from the lack of summer rains, were gloriously abundant. The blueberries, too, offered up a bumper crop, as did the tame, irrigated raspberries. Blackberries, out in the wild, fared poorly, and other crops failed as well under the persistent semi-drought conditions. But my often neglected and ill-tended garden still kept me in salads and soups, stews and gumbos all summer long.

I planted just two hills of sweet potatoes, and some critter came along and pulled one of them up before it could get established. But I dug nearly 20 pounds of heirloom Red Oakleaf yams from the one hill. And a friend who's a better gardener than me harvested more than a hundredweight of Beauregards from a patch not much bigger than a dining room table.

It was an amazing year, all things considered, and now it's being capped by a long, splendid autumn. Actually, I believe our Ozarks autumn is one of these hills' best-kept secrets. Granted, the scenery will not glow so incandescently as the blazing fire reflected from miles of sugar maples, which is the major inspiration for New England bus tours. Here, the colors of the hills blend into a glorious tweed, with the burnt orange of the sassafras, the vermillion of the gum tree, the hickory's bright gold, the butter yellow of catalpa and the blood red sumac (or shoemake, as my grandmother called it) all on a background of caramel, chocolate and cafe au lait of the oak forest. And lest we forget, there is always the understated understory of crimson and russet dogwood, feathery goldenrod, vining bittersweet with its crimson berries and little clumps of fringed lavender where the fall asters grow.

Here's my small offering of wisdom for the season: Get yourself outside. Soak up the scenery. Drink in a last taste of summer's bounty and let it warm your soul. You can worry about feeding all the little ghosts and goblins later. There'll be time enough, soon enough, by the wintertime fire to wonder if you chose the right pepper variety, canned enough applesauce, gathered enough walnuts, put up enough persimmon puree or grew enough garlic. Instead, it's time now to harvest the Ozarks and gather in the beauty of these hills on these too-short autumn days.

NOVEMBER: Imagining into Being

Many years ago, a young friend of mine embroidered what was called a sampler, a saying stitched on cloth, then framed to be hung on the wall of her room. It said, "All things cometh to she who waiteth -- if she worketh like hell while she waiteth." We chuckled over it but I never forgot it. As time went by, I came to see the truth in it. If we're diligent and patient, then we do tend to attract the stuff of our dreams. And certainly, we cannot have the life we cannot imagine.

So it appears to me that if we're smart and spend some serious time focusing on the life we want, we're likely to get at least some version of that life. Of course as my friends in many traditions caution, one should watch what is wished for because it may not come in the form expected.

"Give a care when asking for courage," one said, "or you'll likely get something to be courageous about." Now that's a sobering thought.

But think of the times we've expressed a wish without giving a thought as to the consequences. We can only hope that when that wish went out, the switchboard was closed.

My life has taken some mighty peculiar turns lately, and I've begun looking at all my many little endeavors to see just what might have prompted such turns of events. I think I have it figured out, at least a little.

To understand it, we have to go way back to when I was just a toddler, and my Uncle Tom took great delight in teaching me the words to the popular songs of the day. My favorite was this one.

Far away places with strange-soundin' names
Far away over the sea
Those far away places with the strange-soundin' names
Are callin', callin' me

I start gettin' restless whenever I hear
The whistle of a train
I pray for the day I can get underway
And look for those castles in Spain

They call me a dreamer, well maybe I am
But I know that I'm longin' to see
Those far away places with the strange-soundin' names
They're Callin', callin' me.

Far away places, with strange sounding names. It's been
60-some years since I first sang that song, and I have to
admit I didn't give it much thought in the years between. But
now, out of the blue, as a result of a movie called "Winter's
Bone," I am leaving this week for those very places. Not
Rome. Not Munich. They're far away but familiar and
anyway they're merely cities where I'll change planes. The
real destinations fit the bill much better for me. Torino, for a
film festival. Then, if the powers that be permit, I'll cross the
Caspian, the Aegean and the Black seas to Tbilisi in the
Republic of Georgia for another. Tblisi is in the Caucasus
Mountains, the ancestral home of many of our tree fruits.
Apples, plums, peaches, cherries and pears all originated
there long with the so-called "English" walnut. It's also where
the term Caucasian originated.

If I get there, I'll want to see Tbilisi's botanical gardens.
For they were begun in the fourth century A.D. and they
would be worth the trip all by themselves. I'm also going
with another notion in mind. I want to hear the music and

meet the people. I want to see if they sound like us. Do they sing folk songs? What are they like? Are there any songs about far away places? I hope I get to go over and ask them.

Meanwhile, since this is November and Thanksgiving is just past, I'd like to offer my thanks for this year's many blessings. The first large thank-you goes to Daniel Woodrell, for his splendid novel. Then there's Ann Rosellini and Debra Granik, who saw the movie peeking out from the book, and coaxed it into being. Debra gets another thanks, for her marvelous vision that brought the story to life. My humble gratitude also goes to Executive Producer Jonathan Scheuer for his loving support and for becoming a dear friend to me. And to all the crew and players who built a context to hold the story and the music, and made it get up off the page and walk around, my heartfelt applause to you all. I am honored to have been a part of it, and am blessed beyond measure for what it has brought me.

I hope you don't mind me including you, dear audience, in this burst of gratitude. The very fact that I can natter on about the little things in our little piece of earth and you give me the kindness of listening to me is a never ending source of delight and some bewilderment, for I'm just sharing memories along with some of the things I'm curious about. For instance, when I get to Tbilisi, will I meet folks who, when they imagine far away places with strange sounding names, will they sometimes speak of the Ozarks?

DECEMBER: Tripping the Streets Fantastic

Well, no thanks to their government's most officious bureaucrats, I didn't get to the Republic of Georgia. But I went to Italy with this movie I'm in and am now back safely on home ground. I learned a lot on the trip. For instance, on one of our many long walks down Italian streets, my friend Jonathan Scheuer and I got to talking about the feeling that eventually grabs you by the throat while traveling in far away places.

You know the one, when you look around you and everything feels absolutely alien, and you realize you are very, very far from home. It sneaks up without warning, when you're doing something ordinary -- such as looking for soap. Where does one go in Italy for soap? Now I admit, I wanted something specific. I wanted olive oil soap, because they make it there. It took most of the week to find it. At the mall.

Now, nobody told us about a mall, and in a city built entirely before 1800, we really didn't expect one. I'd been trying the little street-corner markets when I could find one, and when it was open. That's how I learned that stores, most of them, close for lunch. Italians like their lunch. Restaurants who serve it, on the other hand, close up afterwards and stay closed until dinner. In between, you're left with tiny cafes serving coffee and pastries, or odd combinations such as Italian and Japanese. I have a vivid memory of one bleak afternoon in such a place where I washed down some dreadful version of lasagna with bad beer, sitting at a narrow counter, staring at a countertop display of little cuts of what

135

may have been squid. That's when I realized how far from home I had come.

Jonathan got his jolt somewhere else on the street. But jolted we were.

It set me to thinking about how all I need to be comfortable is to find familiar surroundings. Theoretically, all I had to do to find something familiar here was to go to another screening of Winter's Bone.

But I persevered. and finally found my soap at this wonderfully recycled former Fiat factory, with stores built around a giant parking garage-style spiral, where once test drivers drove the brand new little Fiats round and round, up to the roof, where a track would allow them to test the cars at high speeds. I think whoever made up that joke where, in Hell, the engineers are Italian, never saw this place.

Oddly enough, having knocked around for about a week and encountering all manner of things foreign, I got another jolt of realization when returning to a restaurant, this time with a translator who could tell me what I'd been eating. Once we had access to an Italian-speaking intermediary, we discovered that the family who owned the restaurant wanted to know about us, as well.

They'd seen our festival passes and wanted to know what movie we were in and what we did. When we mentioned Winter's Bone, they were thrilled, because it had been written up in the local papers that (Sunday) morning. With these folks, though, it wasn't just the celebrity thing. They knew we weren't international stars. But we had come to their home town from very far away, and they wanted to take this opportunity to make us feel at home.

I had taken the train to the town of Alba the day before, finally getting out of the overwhelmingly stone city and into the countryside. There was a little snow, and the countryside was stark and cold. But behind every villa, every shack and every suburban apartment complex was a garden and a little homemade hoop greenhouse, just like mine.

I understood that language barriers aside, we're all just folks. We have our Ozarks Hills; they have their Alps. I was tickled that the very next day at this little trattoria (which means country-style cafe) I discovered what our far-away neighbors have for Sunday dinner. There was wine from their own little vineyard, served with homemade ravioli filled with roast beef and with the juices as a dressing, a lovely antipasto of grilled eggplant, tomatoes and artichokes, followed by a pear and chocolate tart. It was a far cry from chicken and dumplings, but just as homey. I gave them a CD of the movie soundtrack, and they sent me off with a bottle of homemade wine.

Sometimes I worry about this old world of ours, and the sorry state of human affairs, some of them in far-away places, some close to home. But now, and for the rest of my years, I will have this sweet picture of people in far away places who are not foreign at all, but who have the same love of their Italian hills as we have of our own. It's a good way to start another year.

2011

JANUARY: Big Movie Aftershocks, then Bigger

If it's true that good things, as well as bad, happen in threes, then I'm probably going to just keel over before number three arrives.

I was all primed to tell you about this very big thing that happened in my life, when along came an even bigger one. Now I don't know where to start. So I guess I'll just jump in. As some of you may remember, after the film "Winter's Bone" won the top prize at Sundance, I was invited to attend a film festival in Texas and soon was off on a chain of appearances on behalf of the movie, the last of which took me to Italy.

About the same time, I was asked to join Matt Meacham, Kathleen Morrissey and some others to assist in research to determine if a national heritage area could be established in the central Ozarks of Missouri. I've always been fascinated with the history of this place and this was like receiving the key to the candy store. In the months that followed, I was privileged to visit with literally dozens of unique Ozarks folks, most of them elderly, as they shared their stories and their visions. They described their lives spoke of a tenacity that grew out of finding sustenance in a hard, ancient and beautiful land. One man told of how he'd never been anywhere until he joined the army. On his first night in camp they served brussels sprouts, and he said he felt sorry for them because they'd had such a poor cabbage crop.

Another woman told of how hard life had been in the Depression, and how if those who had more hadn't shared with those who had less, some people would have starved. A third told of how he'd courted his sweetheart down by the gristmill by offering to share a large candy bar. "I suggested we eat it together, starting at each end. We finally made it to the middle, and we've stayed there," he said.

Well, as far as that research was concerned, we got to the middle and went on to the end. We turned in the completed product, a feasibility study based on all sorts of information and observations about Ozarks Culture, and what makes us unlike anywhere else on earth. We're proud of the results and happy that we made the effort. I believe we all see it as one of the more important accomplishments of our lives.

A few days after the study was completed, the second big thing occurred, On a Tuesday morning my phone rang early, around 7:30, while I was still dozing. Before I could answer the call, the other phone started ringing.

Well, I said, something must have happened. I knew the Oscar nominations were due out that day. I didn't think our little movie would get much notice. although I thought it should.

Well, as it happened, and as you've heard, the movie was noticed. The Academy nominated Winter's Bone for best picture, best adapted screenplay, best actress and best supporting actor.

I was floored. Not just because they liked the movie, but because they were shown a realistic picture of a part of life in the Ozarks, warts and all, and they believed it. They were moved. In the end, the story of methamphetamine and its lethal results on families was trumped by the reality, the humility and the nobility of a frontier culture that still exists.

Then I realized that the two stories shared a common theme. Whether you experience the Ozarks through the NHA feasibility study or by watching Winter's Bone. you're getting a glimpse of the real Ozarks. You're not forming your opinions from comic strips with stereotypical characters such as Li'l Abner or Snuffy Smith. There's not a lazy hillbilly to be found, because they're not here, and they never were.

FEBRUARY: Hollywood Hills

This was the segment in which I was interviewed about the experience of going to the Oscars. The trouble was, the interview happened right in the middle of things and I was caught up in the moment and didn't get to say much about the actual experience. My personal experience was that I got to ride out on the train and spend most of a week with an old friend from an earlier life with whom I used to write songs. We got busy during that week and wrote some new ones. Later, at some of the Oscar week parties I got to see a good many of the cast members for the first time since the shoot finished and I stepped back into my ordinary Ozarks world where cancer surgery awaited.

Next in the whirlwind week on the coast was the Independent Spirit Awards, held in a large circus tent on the beach in Marina Del Rey. It was a good idea, but the February weather decided to assert itself. Instead of 70° and breezy, it was mid-50s with on-shore winds whipping the waves to a froth. Most attendees arrived seriously underdressed. Inside, though, it was all smiles as our two unsung stars Dale Dickey and John Hawkes carried off the trophies for Best Supporting Actor and Actress. It was truly heartwarming to witness two people who added so much to the film get their due.

Next day it was the Oscars, which I viewed with the crew, my songwriting partner and Debra's parents. We chose not to do the fancy dress and make up required for those who walk the red carpet. Instead we elected to enjoy less elegant snacks than the smoked salmon in the shape of the Oscar statuette that Debra and Jonathan got, and watched the show on the big-screen TV at the condo. It was splendid, and we were unsurprised at winning no awards. To be nominated was glory enough for all of us.

For me – I never expected something like this to happen in my life. Back in my 20's when I thought I was a real hot shot as a singer, I dreamed that someday I might be famous. But that dream disappeared decades ago. What I took away from this experience was is the marvelous notion that all things come around, that if you're diligent at your craft and practice what you believe, it gets noticed eventually. You get a nod from the universe saying, 'Well done.' I'm happy with that. I don't know if I'll ever be involved with something as splendid again. But if I only get one, this would be the one I'd want.

MARCH: A Fool's Harvest

Long ago on a spring afternoon my mother got the fright of her life when a schoolmate came to the door, shouting that I had been hit by a car as I got off the school bus. I got the surprise of mine when she ran down the street to meet me and gathered me up in her arms. Neither of us heard the other child's cry of April Fool. It was a while before we got over it. Some pranks can go too far.

But April Fool jokes are so irresistible we can hardly resist the temptation. You'd think we'd all be prepared for this bizarre holiday by now. After all, the date's special exemption for random lunacy has been going on for at least 500 years. The Romans had a special celebration about this time in honor of the goddess Hilaria. And some of the pranks, over time, have been truly splendid.

There was the 1998 Burger King advertisement of the "Left-Handed Whopper," in which all the sandwich ingredients had been rotated 180 degrees. Several thousand people across the U.S. went in to request one, and some requested the "right hand version."

In 1957, the British Broadcasting Company offered a straight-faced report on the quality of that year's spaghetti harvest. Enough people believed it that for a few weeks, local nurseries were plagued with requests for prices on small spaghetti trees.

One of my favorites was an elaborate hoax concocted by British astronomer Patrick Moore, who announced that at 9:47 a.m. on a certain day, a once-in-a-lifetime astronomical event was going to occur. The planet Pluto would pass behind Jupiter, temporarily causing a gravitational alignment that would counteract and lessen the Earth's own gravity. Moore told his listeners that if they jumped in the air at the exact moment that this planetary alignment occurred, they would experience a strange floating sensation. When 9:47 a.m. arrived, BBC2 began to receive hundreds of phone calls from listeners claiming to have felt the sensation. One woman even reported that she and her eleven friends had risen from their chairs and floated around the room.

It appears the impulse to play the practical joke is so strong that people can go to ridiculous lengths to pull it off. In 1974: residents of Sitka, Alaska were alarmed when the nearby, long-dormant volcano, Mount Edgecumbe, appeared suddenly to come to life. It began to belch out billows of black smoke and people spilled out of their homes onto the streets to gaze up at the volcano, terrified that it was active again and might soon erupt. That was exactly the intention of local practical joker Porky Bickar, who for reasons known only to himself and to God, had used his little airplane to fly hundreds of old tires up into the volcano's crater and then set them on fire. The hoax was so successful that, according to local legend, when Mount St. Helens erupted six years later, a Sitka resident wrote to Bickar to tell him, "This time you've gone too far!"

We just can't seem to resist.

Just 11 years ago, in 2000, a news release sent to the media stated that the 15th annual New York City April Fool's Day Parade was scheduled to begin at noon on 59th Street and would proceed down to Fifth Avenue. Hundreds of people turned out to watch because of the extraordinary floats that were described. But after standing in the cold a couple of hours, they realized they'd been had.

Pranksterism is not an impulse known only to Anglo-Saxons. In 1915, in the midst of World War I, a French aviator flew over a German camp and dropped what appeared to be a huge bomb. The German soldiers immediately scattered in all directions, but no explosion followed. After some time, the soldiers crept back and gingerly approached the bomb. They discovered it was actually a large football with a note tied to it that read, "April Fool!"

Then there was the Australian television station that ran a segment about the "Dial-O-Fish," a new electronic fishing rod that could be set to catch any desired species. A "fishing expert" demonstrated how to use the device. First he dialed up garfish and soon had caught half a dozen. Next he dialed up an orange roughy. Hundreds of viewers reportedly called in wanting to know where they could buy the rod, and a Japanese manufacturer declared it was ready to go into production immediately

Neither is Russia immune. In 1994, reporters from The Moscow Tribune went out onto the streets of Moscow to ask people what they thought about the ethnic cleansing in Brutistan. They received a variety of concerned replies, a remarkable occurrence, given that Brutistan does not exist.

Sometimes, the joke is so good and so obvious that people catch onto it, only the joke itself doesn't exist. For instance, in one Missouri town on April first, folks who got a summons for jury duty saw the joke immediately, and no one showed up. Only it wasn't a joke. Deputy sheriffs had to go to their homes, gather them up and haul them to the courthouse. They don't call this the Show-me State for nothing.

I think my favorite of all, though, happened in 1992 when the The Hollywood Park Racetrack in Los Angeles placed an 85-foot banner on the ground with a message in 20-foot-high letters. It could only be seen from the air. But the racetrack is just beside the flight path of the Los Angeles International Airport, a perfect spot to catch the eye of incoming airline passengers as they descended into the landing strip. It read, "Welcome to Chicago."

Don't be surprised if the Goddess Hilaria shows up on your doorstep on April Fool's Day with a poke in the ribs or a tale too good, or wild, to be true. Tis the season, even in these Ozarks hills.

APRIL: Weathering the Weather

When it rains, they say, it pours, and so it has been in this month of showers, storms and floods. The Ozarks has a history of hard times and hardscrabble survival, and weather is implicated in more than one of the mischief-makers. The ice storms, the illnesses, the sudden blow of accident or violence that may happen to one or two, but that shakes a family and often a whole community. Later, in a time and place far removed, we look back on those times as well as happier ones, and call them a trip down memory lane. There's a lot of that happening this week, in between watching the weather radar and listening for news of our neighbors near and far. I came near to being one of those stories myself, heading home in a rainstorm and not realizing how heavy the downpour really had been just before I ventured out in it.

I was coming home from a free local Rounders gig at the Senior Center in a blinding rainstorm when I came within a hair of being washed away down Howell Creek. Choosing a route I had driven hundreds of times, the most recent being early that evening, I drove into deep water before I knew it. I was a hundred yards from the bridge that spanned the creek bed on what I thought was a level section of road. But I was disoriented by the rain, the lightning, and the sets of headlights coming toward me. I didn't realize the creek had come out if its banks, and the headlights were of cars that had turned around and were trying to escape. I'm still not exactly sure what saved me, except I was lucky to keep the engine running as I fought the current of the rushing creek and the wake churned up by passing cars, the last one of which threw a wave of muddy water over the hood of my little Geo. By then I could no longer tell where the street was except a little ahead I could see a street sign. I kept gunning the engine as it choked and sputtered until I reached a point where I could turn into the side street. The water was as high but the current less, and so I kept on, with engine coughing and clutch slipping and unidentified debris clunking away at the undercarriage and gradually worked my way free.

I waited another two hours, drinking fast food coffee and listening to others tell stories of close calls before the water receded on all the roads enough for me to get home. An exciting night, but not one I'll want to repeat soon. The odd part, if we can forget my longtime addiction to adrenaline, is that I wasn't even a little scared when it was happening. I was too busy telling myself to focus, focus and find the next thing to do. It's only afterward that I replay that wave coming over the hood and up the windshield, and realize how close I came to deeper waters than I'm ready to try.

MAY: Singing Along the Traces

Lately I've done nothing but pack clothes, study maps and muse over metaphors highways, journeys and trails – all prompted by the fact that my little band of troubadours from the movie "Winter's Bone" is about to head out on a national tour to showcase our new album of songs and also promote the movie's soundtrack. I'd been so busy making ready for the trip that until now, I hadn't thought much about or destinations.

We have many names for the paths we travel, from trails to sidewalks, from byways to freeways. In earlier times, though, before technology and advanced paving materials, most paths were made by walking. When enough walkers walked long enough, those paths became indelible. Back then, we called them Traces.

The more famous ones from those times include the Natchez Trace, the Bienville Trace, the Tunica Trace, and the Atakapa. But there are thousands more such paths, traceable and untraced, from the long, long history of this land's occupation by a multitude of tribes. In my own back yard, growing up, I was amazed to find the indented pattern of an X marking the crossing of two old wagon roads, long before a town was eventually built and the trails made way for streets. At week's end, this unlikely band of travelers will head north and west along the most well-established modern roads in the U.S. and a little bit of Canada. We'll be taking our own blend of Ozarks music and fun out to the people who live in that vast, incomprehensible land that we call "Off," as in "He's not from here. He's from off."

While we were making travel arrangements I suddenly realized this was, apart from the music, about to be a personal journey for me. You see, along with my parents, I was once among those emigrant outmigrants who helped make some of those trails and traces across the western prairies, over the mountains and along the western coast. I've long ago lost track of the number of trips we made back and forth, out to a job and back home; me, my mother and my traveling electrician father.

That was a long time ago. This trip on the western roads will be my first in 35 years. To the northwest it will be 50 years or more. Will I remember any of it? Will the things I remembered be gone? Mostly, I remember the mountains. And the vast gorge of the Columbia. And going out with my Osage uncle once in Washington State to purchase smoked salmon from members of a tribe I'm not sure I ever knew the name of. And being served meals in which meats like elk and bear were a prominent feature. I'm not sure I'll be able to get anywhere near those experiences again. But perhaps if I'm lucky, I'll find traces.

More familiar will be the drive down the coast from Oregon through California, where I lived for about a decade. We'll spend two days on that drive, hoping to still have time for an afternoon in that grand harlot of a city, San Francisco. Perhaps we'll have some crab at the wharf, buy some chocolate, ride a cable car and search out piroshkis on Russian Hill. Then we'll hit the trail at sunrise, L.A. bound, through the fields of broccoli, brussel sprouts and artichokes of the central coast to the orange and avocado groves of the southland.

Then it's a long hop across the desert, up through Texas, a stop in Tulsa for lunch with relatives and home in time for the Old Time Music festival in West Plains. A week later, we'll do it all again, heading east, via Nashville and Atlanta to the coast, up to New York, over to Chicago, St. Louis and

Kansas City, by way of Minneapolis. I'm sure I'll have stories to share for months to come.

We plan to do our best to leave our mark and a few CDs along the way. And certainly the journey will leave its mark on us. All along the way, I'll be searching for traces of my life of long ago. But one thing I know. When I reach the end of this journey, I'll return knowing that there's no place on earth like these Ozarks Hills.

JUNE: Joplin

As a child living in rural Barry County, I thought that
Joplin, Missouri was the gateway to the wild frontier It was a
good place to visit, people said, but you wouldn't want to
live there. It was a little too wild for the tastes of my older
relatives. The younger ones, now, including my mother,
could tell tales of the dances attended, the parties invited to,
the drives in their '34 Fords, a little beyond safe
surroundings. Just past Joplin was the Indian Country of
Oklahoma, the Kansas wheat harvest, the way west. In my
mind the word Joplin only needed to be uttered, and I was
away on fantastic voyages full of danger and delight.

As I grew up I came to see that the town at the western
edge of the Ozarks was just a town, not the fabled city of my
imagination. Still, I wondered what it was about this place
that conjured up so many tales. So I did some research that
put feet on a few fables and eliminated others from my
mind. One myth my research refuted was that the town was
named after ragtime musician Scott Joplin. Or he for it.
Instead, I found that the name came from where they put the
town – on the banks of Joplin Creek. The creek was named
for the Rev. Harris Joplin, an early settler and frontier
preacher who opened his creekside wilderness home to
share the gospel, officiate at the occasional wedding or lay a
soul to rest. He founded the first Methodist congregation in
the area.

Joplin's first settlement began after deposits of lead were
found along the creek. After the Civil War, miners also
discovered zinc ore. Prices soared, and by 1873, the boom

town of Joplin was being called "Jack City" for its vast reserve of zinc ore. The drive to mine zinc was on. By the time the source was tapped out, more than 70 percent of the area that would become the modern city of Joplin was undermined with tunnels and shafts. The city on the edge of the plains had gone from frontier town to a regional metropolis, with had railroads, trolleys, opera houses, and the infamous House of Lords. This Main Street establishment offered fine dining on the first floor, gambling on the second and a third floor reserved for what was termed "female companionship."

The city's reputation for behavior outside the boundaries of good taste was capped during the Depression when two area lawmen were killed trying to flush the famed outlaw couple, "Bonny and Clyde," from their hideout in a Joplin apartment. Today that apartment is on the National Register of Historic Places and offers tours and the occasional sleepover.

Joplin is also the hometown of such notables as poet and writer Langston Hughes, actor Dennis Weaver and criminal evangelist Tony Alamo. Mickey Mantle played minor-league baseball there, and Thomas Hart Benton once drew cartoons for the local paper.

Tragically, the city also has another, darker history – of calamitous weather. The area at the edge of the southern plains is known, for good reason, as tornado alley. Its path is wide and covers most of the Ozarks. But Joplin is at its unfortunate center. Those stunned by the most recent damage should know that the city has been hit no fewer than four times previously. The first tornado struck the fledgling city in 1873. The next hit in 1902, heavily damaging much of the town, including the new St. John's Hospital. The city rebuilt, only to be struck again in 1908. Then, for decades, there was a reprieve. Several storms struck nearby, but Joplin was spared.

Then in 1971, the reprieve ended. A twister struck the same exact area that was demolished in this most recent storm, but was smaller, and killed just one while injuring 50. Then another reprieve of 37 years before a massive storm passed within 10 miles of the city in 2008.

But nothing could have prepared the city for the evil winds of 2011– the worst ever, surpassing all.The massive EF5 multiple-vortex tornado that struck Joplin on the afternoon of Sunday, May 22 will go down as the eighth worst storm since records have been kept. Altogether 163 people died and countless were injured. St. John's Regional Health Center this time was destroyed beyond repair.

And what are the people of Joplin doing? They're rebuilding. It started the next day.

Just like Arthur Cox did, who owned of Cox Baseball Park, when it was destroyed in the 1902 tornado. He managed to get debris cleared from the field within 24 hours, because there was a game scheduled, he said. And by golly, they played.

And so Joplin, that rowdy frontier town and city of fable, is growing once again, Phoenix- like, from the ashes, aided by neighbors near and far. In doing so it has once again become a living example of the resilience, resourcefulness and pure gumption of the stouthearted folks who populate these Ozarks Hills. While we mourn those lost and grieve the passing of so much history, we salute our Ozarks friends and neighbors who have survived the ravages of time and weather, as they go about another rebirth of the once-and-future fabled city of Joplin.

JULY: Hotter than Heck

My little band of musicians has just came in from a national tour, where we spent considerable time driving across the country. Everywhere we went the weather was hot.

The southern part of the trip was the worst, causing me to reflect on that long ago quote by Sen. Sam Nunn of Georgia, who said the only two things that made the South tolerable at all were civil rights and air conditioning. We, too, were grateful for civil rights but equally grateful that the Chevy van that carried us through the tour had good air, front and back. We just dialed up the mix we wanted, and it was delivered.

Once we came home, of course, it was July, and we expected it to be hotter than blue blazes. As I turned on the air full blast at my home, I wondered if I hadn't been complaining a little too much. Over all, I had managed to be comfortable for most of the whole tour. And I'm grateful for my comforts at home, because I'm old enough to remember when life was different. For my garden's sake, I am grateful for a good well because I won't, please god, have to say those words over my garden that I heard so often in my Ozarks childhood, "The garden was good until July, then it just dried up."

I also remember the days before indoor plumbing. In the 1950s in rural Missouri, the well was just a pipe sunk far down in the earth, into which fit a well bucket, a long, narrow tube with a trap at the bottom that opened when it hit the water level. It filled as it sank, and closed as it was drawn up, holding the water in. Once it was drawn up, you held it over a two-gallon water bucket and pulled up a finger-sized ring attached to a slender steel rod and opened the trap, filling the bucket. Your water depended on how many times the bucket went down and was pulled back up.

That's how it was in those days of minimal, mechanical technology. My family's well was 150 feet deep and fed by a good water source, so the water came up to within 60 feet of the top. The rope that attached to the bucket was about 75 feet. To get a bucket of water to drink or cook with, the two-pound bucket had to be lowered on 65 feet of rope in order to submerge the entire bucket. Then the 20 or so pounds of water, bucket and rope had to be pulled back up, using a pulley hung from a tripod about six feet off the ground. One of the tripod's arms held a large horse shoe nailed to it on which the coils of rope could be hung.

Just to wash the dishes, a second bucket was drawn to be heated on the stove. A third bucket was required for the rinse. To wash a load of clothes meant filling both the washer and the rinse tub with 20 gallons of water each. Of course in those days, under those circumstances, one didn't wash every load in clean water. That would have been frivolous. Instead, the wash water was heated, either on the kitchen stove or a little wood-burning "laundry stove" outside the back door, using a wash boiler, a tall, oblong pan that held about three buckets of water.

Into the first load, in the hottest water, went the whites - the sheets, Dad's Sunday shirts, etc. The second load in lukewarm was for light weight colors - Mom and Granny's clothes, the underwear, handkerchiefs and such. By the time those were finished, the wash water was gray, so more soap and another two buckets of hot water were added. Then it was time to add the work clothes, the denims and heavy khakis, the overalls, the socks.

Each piece, as it came from the washer, went through the wringer, an apparatus that forced the clothing between two rubber rollers, one on springs so it could give a little for heavy items or for buttons and into the rinse tub. Each item was dipped into and out of the rinse water several times to remove the soap, then passed back through the wringer to remove as much water as possible. It was then collected in a basket. While the next load was washing, the basket was carried out to the clothesline, which was usually hung between two trees or tall posts, and fastened to the line with pins, either the ones you've seen, the two slats of wood fastened together with a strong spring, or the older style, a single, slotted piece of wood often called a peg. When dry, the clothes were brought inside and either dampened and rolled up to await the iron, or folded and put away.

Before the last load of work clothes came out, the rinse tub was emptied and refilled with another 20 gallons of water, making a total of 32 buckets of water, or about 640 pounds of water, bucket and rope, hauled up every washday, not counting the four or five buckets that day for drinking, cooking, tea and coffee making and the bath you'd want after a summer day of laundry

That's how it was in the 50s, in rural Missouri. Knowing that, as I do because I was there in that time and it was my job to draw the water, causes me to reflect on how life is now here in the land of plenty for most of us, and how it is in other places where not even clean water can be counted on, much less your own water source, or indoor plumbing, or a water heater, or air conditioning, or civil rights.

I am grateful beyond words for the insights of age which remind me that today In These Ozarks Hills, without a thought as to how effortless are my comforts, I am able to water my garden, use the spin cycle, take a shower with the turn of a tap, and turn up the air a bit when it gets muggy.

AUGUST: It Runs in the Family

Have you noticed how many times a trade or a profession will run in a family over years, generations sometimes? Sometimes it's tied to the family name. I can't tell you how many carpenters and woodworkers I've known whose names are Sawyer, Woods, Oakley and, well, Carpenter.

That may be the reason for so many Smiths, since the word is also a suffix to a number of other designations of a trade, like blacksmith, silversmith, wordsmith, etc.

But sometimes a trade will attach to a family, or vice versa, and just not let go. For instance, in my mother's family a good many of us attached ourselves to the postal service. My mother was a postmaster, as was her mother, her father and her uncle, all at the same little rural post office at Butterfield, over in Barry County. My mother's sister married a man who was a mail carrier, and their son became a mail carrier as well.

For a while it became almost a calling, and it was implied that if I ever straightened up and came home, I could be a postmaster too. Of course that's not the way it worked out.

But here lately, what with the movie, and the soundtrack, and the radio show, and the printed version of the radio pieces, and with a new CD just out and an expanded version of the essays on its way, it seems I may be coming back into the fold, but in a brand new way.

I keep getting posts on social media sites. I have a blog, and I do Facebook. I haven't yet gone in for MySpace or

Twitter, and I probably won't. I mean, who has time for all that chatter? Perhaps when I was younger and had more to say, or believed I had, it would have been more worth diving in and just trying them all. But these days I'm lucky I get to the end of the week without being farther behind than when I started. With that plan, I expected to be able to keep up.

But the blog thing turned into a monster when people who watched the movie and liked the music learned they could write in and talk about it or read about it, and the movie, and me. Since its creation in June of last year, just over 71,000 people have elected to do that. Most just dropped by and read a little and didn't comment. But I've had to answer a lot of mail over the last year, enough to make me want to give up the whole endeavor, except for one thing.

Old friends, people I thought I'd never hear from again, have been popping up, one or two at a time. People from high school. From California, where I spent a decade before returning home. And people I've never heard of before, but from all parts of the globe. Yesterday it was a woman in Bangladesh. The day before, Australia. Last week, two from the British Isles, one in Scotland, the other in Wales, the week before, Norway. And just today, someone wrote that I was sure I'd never hear from again. Someone with whom I'd had a falling out after a long friendship, and nursed a grudge about for a long time. "I know we parted on bad terms," they said. "But I am happy for your success. It would be astounding and fun to hear from you."

And then they told me about their life from then until now, and it was only then that I realized how long it had been. All that heat and bad feelings were nearly 40 years ago. Surely it was time to set it aside. And so I did, and answered the letter, filled in the blanks caused by separation, and offered thanks for their courage in trying to set things right.

I might well have thanked them also for heading my thoughts in this odd direction, from postmasters to web masters. It's all a part of the long history of our trying to maintain, create or repair relationships with those who make our lives fuller. I think back now to those earlier times, when I would write home to the folks and just address the letter to Postmaster, Butterfield Missouri. Or when I went off to seek my fortune in California and wound up working for a publisher who had me editing manuscripts from the ends of the globe, and I'd snip the stamps off the packaging and send them home to add to my mother's stamp collection.

Everything's changed, and yet, not all that much. Far away has gotten closer, that's all. That, and I have three post office boxes now – one in West Plains, one out by the road across from the farm, and one right here on my computer. Some days they're all full, and I'm like my mother, muttering and singing and fussing my way through all the deliveries until they're sorted out. It's become part of what I do, and it's a good trade, one I can practice without having to go too far, too often, from these Ozarks Hills.

SEPTEMBER: Another Rich Harvest

Autumn has come to the Ozarks. The change in the air tells us more surely than the date on the calendar. 'Tis the season of harvest and of loss, endings and abeyances, clothing that was proper for the heat of summer now slid to the side on the closet rack, making way for the colors and fabrics of fall.

As always at this time of year, my thoughts turn both outward and inward, out to the fields and forests where the last bounty awaits; and inward to the deepening of thoughts and messages contained in the waning light, the tempered warmth and the lessening of days. The apple harvest is in full swing at area orchards, and fresh cider has arrived on the shelves at the grocer's. Homes that have apple trees or access to them are awash in the scent of apple butter, apple pie and the clear jars of apple jelly, like summer sunshine stored on the shelves.

For those of us who can look beyond their gnarly shapes and weathered skins, the splendid bounty of hard pears from old Ozarks pear trees is also a gift, and in some homes the choice is not between pears and no pears, but between pear smoothies, pear jam, which is called pear honey for its taste, and the rows of little jars filled with what looks like nothing other that canned little slices of the crescent moon. I'd like some of each, please.

It's the lovely season of the tree fruits, those we cherish and those that go unnoticed. I'm in the rare position of having one end of my car thumped on by black walnuts falling and the other end being whacked by falling buckeyes. The walnuts are a chore to crack but worth their weight in gold, while the buckeyes, I mean, what do you do with them.

Back in the days when we relied more on nature's bounty than the wonderful world of chemistry and petroleum byproducts, buckeyes were ground to a paste that was called, aptly, library paste, and used to repair books. Now, they're mostly in demand by squirrels, who find them a tasty and easily shucked alternative to the walnuts, whose hard green husks are still firmly attached, and are almost surely evil-tasting and besides, they turn their chins black.

Buckeyes are unappetizing to humans, so since the chinquapins are mostly gone, we'll wait for the walnuts or find some excuse to wander south a ways in search of those fat southern pecans.

The wise foragers know the local pecans, while smaller, are rich in flavor. It has become remarkably hard to worm the location of the best trees out of those folks, although sometimes a trade will work. For instance, I have a source for red fall raspberries. But I can't think of anything more delicious this time of year, so I probably won't be trading any. In fact, it was probably mean to bring it up.

And then there's persimmons, those wonderful red-orange globes so delicious after a frost and so deceitful, looking ripe long before they are, and offering their own mean trick instead of a treat for the unwary. But we love them anyway. One of my favorite things on early morning autumn walks, is to search for persimmon trees, which on misty fall mornings are sometimes so full of fruit they can turn the very air around them into the incandescent orange of small, glowing suns.

Autumn, here at last, and never more welcome than after such a hellishly hot summer as this has been. Certainly the months past have been hard for other reasons than the heat, with jobs and homes lost, the economy in tatters and dissent everywhere you look.

But for me, upon reflection, the best antidote to the dark thoughts that can certainly arise from dwelling on the times is to choose to dwell instead on how reliable is the inevitable turning of seasons, and what that means; how each turning offers a new view as it casts aside the old.

Time passes, and with it the passing of things, conditions, and of those we love, or in some instances those we hope to outlast. As someone who is now experiencing another corner turning, from middle age to what's termed the elder years, I must also acknowledge that the view from here is at once daunting and still full of promise. I, too, am coming into the autumn of my years, and I daily find reasons to treasure the experience, mostly.

Yes, the body continues its journey, becoming more frail and yet not so much, really. And the person who abides there seems most days to be at once more forgetful and more aware, more appreciative, more alive. Aging is a metaphor, of course, one perhaps more easily seen in these ancient hills that have seen more seasons than a human can imagine.

You don't think so? Imagine, then, the world before there were forests of oak and hickory, when the springs were bubbling pools of lead and zinc and the mountains were tall, majestic, and utterly alien. We can't. These forests were here to welcome the first tread of a human foot, the first population of elk and otter, the first harvest. The seasons were here long before us, and will far outlast us. What a recurring revelation, that these mountains' heart will continue to beat, long after ours come to rest. Seasons, like problems, and persimmons, and people we love or endure, will pass, as will we.

Here lives the promise of these Ozarks Hills, that they will ever await those who will come after, bringing new growth after the rest and renewal of winter, ever flowing into a summer of abundance and trial, toward yet another season of harvest.

OCTOBER: Into the Long Dark

October's end has a special meaning in a number of
cultures. In some, it marks the end of the old year and the
start of the new. In others, it is believed that the veil between
the worlds is at its thinnest point, and voices of loved ones
can be heard across the void. In about every case, at least in
the northern hemisphere, October in the natural world is the
month of the first frost, the first killing freeze, the migration
of birds and those RV owners dubbed by southerners the
"snowbirds," and for those who stay at home, the journey
into the long dark. No wonder, then, that the pagan
celebration of All Hallows Eve has migrated down the ages
into the celebration of Halloween, with all its spooks and
goblins and playful mischief. A last outing, perhaps, before
the cold sets in and makes an evening by the fire seem the
most attractive. In a few months, the hopeful gardeners will
be perusing the new seed catalogs. But for now, we're still
covering the tender herbs, hoping for one more fragrant
harvest, and trying to find places to put all those freshly dug
sweet potatoes and that pile of green tomatoes rescued just
before the thermometer hit the freeze mark. This year I had
to have someone do that for me, not because of illness this
time, but because I'm away from home, city-bound, and
having to grab the change of seasons in small doses, out the
windows of trains, cars and hotels. Not for me this month
the long walks in the woods and creekside musings. They'll
keep.

Still, you can't help, or at least I can't, feeling the change to
jacket weather, the crisp snap of the breeze, the early
nightfall. It always takes me to the same place, the place of
endings, evening's last light, the first hint of winter in the air,
and the summing up of life's many lessons. I retain the

image in my mind from long ago, when my age could be measured in single digits and I was out on an evening's adventure. The small street light across from our house in the village was outshone by October's full moon, and I could see my breath in the air. I was out prowling the field behind the house and spotted a rabbit's trail through the weeds and into a tangle of buckbrush and wild honeysuckle. On impulse, and properly clad in rough jeans and a farmer's jacket, I went to my knees and onto my side, getting my head down far enough to peer down the travel-worn lane. At once my perspective shifted, and I seemed to be looking down a long, arched tunnel with high trees soaring above and the end lost somewhere in darkness. Then just as suddenly, it seemed the metaphor became real, and I was looking at the journey my life must take, down a solitary path, with destination unknown. Certainly no one knows on the issuance of the ticket where the destination might be, or how soon we'll arrive. I'd prefer mine to be still some several stops away. But to think that I was looking then at a road whose end is a little past now, and I was excited then at the prospect of adventures, and discoveries, and all the twists and turns my life would take as it followed after all those rabbit tracks. And I still am. Life offers many challenges and more blessings, and a few of what I've called "difficult gifts," as with the loss of a friend or family member, or the sad end to a valued relationship, or seeing friends battle the discomforts and debilities of age. Some kinds of knowledge are dearly bought, but so far, always worth more than they cost. We only value these things that are important to us, and sometimes we realize their importance after they are gone. But if you are lucky, you eventually reach an age where, knowing the cost and weighing the value, you'd pay it again, without question. Such are the musings of a coot such as this old hillbilly under the October moon who, no matter how far the travels, always manages to keep one foot in these Ozarks Hills.

NOVEMBER: Fortune Shining Down

If you're listening to this live on a Friday morning, you're either on your way to work at one of those jobs that don't let you have a four-day weekend, or you've finally made it inside one of the big box stores and you're hoping that keeping your attention on NPR on your iPod will ward off a panic attack as you're watching someone carry off what might be your last chance at a new TV.

If you're extremely lucky, you're sitting at home enjoying your morning coffee, thinking about dismantling the remains of yesterday's turkey and sending good wishes to your son, daughter, nephew or spouse who is braving the crowd waiting for that TV.

If fortune is shining down upon you, you and everyone to whom you'd send good wishes are very happy with the TVs they have and you are sticking to thoughts of turkey leftovers, and anyone they might have forgotten to thank

I was going over my list last night when up popped someone, or a group of someones, I hadn't thought of in quite a while. They're all long gone from this plane, and exist only as fond memories of a teacher, relative or friend we once knew and still think the world of.

I never knew them in the classroom, nor did I know any of them long enough or well enough for them to count me as a friend. Even so, I became a confidante, and the secret they told me will stay with me always. And since they've all gone on, I guess it's ok for me to share it with you. Some years back, the son of a former teacher, Pauline Smith Pond, engaged me to help his mother write her life story. She had taught in many one-room schools in earlier days and had many tales to tell of her experiences. As I got to know her, I was impressed with not just her quick memory but her delightful sense of humor and her lighthearted description of times which must have been very hard as she was growing up and helping her family make its way in the world. At one point she told me "I may have grown up, but I'll never be a lady because when I laugh, it doesn't come out a laugh. I still just giggle like a silly girl." I'd heard her laugh and knew what she meant, but I found it charming, just like her stories. One story she told was about her brother, Bernard, who had set his mind on getting a degree in education, so that he could become qualified to be a school administrator. His grades were excellent, and he had applied to a small college in Carthage, Mo. and they offered him a scholarship. The trouble was, he had no money to make the trip. So he took his small savings, tied his suitcase to the back of his bicycle, and pedaled away, headed from West Plains to Carthage. This was in the 1930s, and the road from West Plains to Mountain Grove had not yet been paved; it was all rocks and tall hills. By the time he reached Mtn. Grove, he realized he could not continue that way. So he took what money he had, put his suitcase on the bus, and rode his bicycle the rest of the way.

Good heavens, I said as Pauline finished the tale. That's almost unbelievable. She laughed. No, she said, That's just gumption. It's what you have to have if you're going to make it in this world. Well, she was right, I thought, but still...

Time went by, and I mentioned to my older friends that I had heard an amazing story about Bernard Smith. Oh yes, they said. And he came back home and made a fine administrator. He worked all around this area for years. Well, I was impressed. I knew where Carthage was, and I realized I'd find the trip tiring if I made it by car.

Then on the Sunday after Thanksgiving that year, I stopped by to visit Pauline and see if she was in the mood to tell me stories. But she had company. Her sister was there, and her brother, Bernard, and his wife. They all had stories to tell, and I spent a lovely afternoon just listening. But the afternoon grew late, and as I started to excuse myself, they all said, yes, it's late. We must be going, too. It will be dark soon. Yes, said Bernard, and it's hard enough for us to navigate in the daylight since I've gone blind. I started to laugh at the obvious joke. But no one laughed with me. Instead, they all looked embarrassed. Pauline put her hand up to her mouth and her sister said, Now don't you start. But soon they were all laughing, and Pauline said, You might as well tell her. The secret's out.

The truth was, Bernard really had lost his sight as a result of macular degeneration. He could only see a little bit, out at the corners. Worse, he was the only one of them who could drive. But how else were they to get to the nursing home on Sundays to visit Pauline.

I don't know whose idea it was because they were all talking at once. but here's the gist of it.

Every Sunday, when they figured everyone had gone to church and come home, the three would get in the car, Bernard behind the wheel, his wife snuggled up next to him, and his sister in the back seat, leaning over his left shoulder. He drove and they gave him constant feedback, if he was too fast or too slow, too far left or right, and when to turn corners. Fortunately, although they lived four miles out of town, there were only four corners to manage, and they were all right turns, they told me..

When they finished talking and swearing me to secrecy, they sat back, looking remarkably pleased with themselves. It was absolutely loony. But here they were, this little, gumption-filled family, all in their 80s except for Pauline, who was 92. She was their big sister. They weren't about to leave her there alone without company. And so they continued for many more Sundays, until Pauline was gone. They never had an accident; they were never found out.

But now, with another thanksgiving past, when I think about the years ahead and how I'll move my way into that section of life they call the declining years, I only have to think about the Smith family and their unwavering courage, their valor, their gumption. And I am grateful forever that they merrily pointed the way forward. Here's wishing you as the holidays progress the gift of gumption. It's what you have to have if you're going to make it in this world. It's not available in stores.

DECEMBER: Time to Turn the Page

This month, I was all set to launch a light-hearted episode about how this was the year when very nearly every story we hadn't heard the end of - ended. Bin Laden, the end. War in Iraq. Ended. The12-thousand year old Mayan Calendar - zip. Even Khaddafi - Kaput. It's gotten to where the news has to be gigantic in order to even make the paper. Or the broadcast. And I think most of us can probably do without any more news of epic proportions for a little while. Still, it would have made a great story. But then, when I least expected it, my consciousness was jogged by the unlikely and somewhat ludicrous sight of a tiny Smart car whizzing down the road in front of me, smartly adorned in reindeer antlers.

And it occurred to me it might be time to look into some notions that, although no less important, are somewhat less epic in nature. It is the holidays, after all. And on that subject, I was already trying to process two observations recently made by friends that have set my head to thinking. The first was a comment last week by a friend as a Christmas song played on the radio. "Every night when a child is born is a holy night," she said. And I had to admit it was true. Then just this morning another friend posted on Facebook the suggestion that we replace the i in the word holiday with a y, making this a season full of holy days. Another true thing. The more I thought about it, the more holy days came to mind, and I started making a list. The day a daughter leaves for the battlefield. The day a son comes home. The night we say goodbye to a friend as well as the one when we say hello to a newborn. The evening a struggling student accepts a hard-earned diploma. The morning a brilliant coworker accepts an award. Well, you see how it can just go on.

It also makes it difficult to assign the idea of holiness to just one set of beliefs, or group of believers. I mean, the whole notion of parking your holiday season right on the Solstice, when the darkest night passes in the northern hemisphere and the longest day begins in the south, means that we, as earthlings, celebrate the change in virtually every culture and every land, every language and creed. The Christmas tree, the Yule Log, the Hanukkah lights, all symbolize renewal, reaffirmation, resolve.

Given all that, it's also difficult to ignore the fact that there are far more things that unite us as humans than things that divide.

It also suggests that in addition to the large things that have happened, we may be on the verge of even larger opportunities. Consider the Arab Spring, followed by the American Autumn. People coming together in larger numbers and with fewer instances of violence than at any time I can recall. Are we nearing a point where we can actually begin to consider the issues that affect us all? Is it possible, here at the turning of the world, that we might decide to stop fighting over the small stuff, the spoils, the upper hand, and instead put our considerable energy as planetary neighbors into dealing with the big and universal challenges that lay ahead for us all, like climate change, world hunger, loss of arable land, the poisoning of the oceans, and yes, even the possibility of solar storms that have the potential to throw us iPhone and Android dependent sophisticates right back into the mechanical age? Might we stop talking about leveling the playing field and just do it? I'm not sure that's a game we're all eager to play. But it does tend to put things into proper perspective. We have discovered, or at least have become aware of the past decade, that, for instance, We don't need a war to prove that we all bleed the same color. We don't need to ruin things to discover what we can't do without. We don't need to suffer loss to know how our neighbors feel.

So about that calendar. What if, instead of signifying the end of the world, it means it's time to turn the page? Take up a new set of tools. Build a future that works better for everyone, not just those with the most toys. You might say it would take a miracle. But heck, we're no stranger to miracles. The very fact that this earth keeps spinning its wobbly way through space is miracle enough to share at this holy, star-filled moment and at every moment. No matter what damage we humans continue to inflict, it just keeps going round and round. Celebrate that along with the beliefs of your faith. It doesn't get any holier than this.

Here's wishing you and all our neighbors on this tiny speck of earth in the midst of a vast darkness, the holiest of holidays full of light and promise, whatever your tradition or your address.

2012

JANUARY: In the land of Not Yet

There's nothing quite like the wind keening up high in the trees as an Arctic front approaches to let you know that winter has finally arrived. We'll break out our stock of ancient phrases and mutter things like "It will be no fit night to be abroad." as we pour a toddy or a draught of tea. Deep mid-Winter is unmistakable, a time not measured by instruments. We feel it in our bones. Old bones especially. This is when many spry seniors begin to realize that even the best of exercise and nutrition and attitudes can only hold off the years for so long. And even the 30-somethings begin to yearn for their own younger days when air pressure drops and joints begin to creak and complain.The old timers have a phrase for it. "As the days lengthen, the cold strengthens." And so it is. Grateful as we may be for the comforts of enough wood, sufficient propane, dependable electricity to keep warm, this is the time we must also reflect that it doesn't have to be so; that for many even in this, the richest land, some will do without, and more will, if the storm worsens.

Welcome, then, to the dark of the year, when many with better sense than these frail humans have burrowed deep within their covers in their dens and won't peek out until the worst is past. I'm with them.

I do my best to hibernate during these shortest days, even though I have to stay focused enough to feed the wood stove, wind the mantle clock and fetch the dog's breakfast. But it's a fine season for napping, and conjuring up splendidly prophetic or downright silly dreams. Even though they were massacred a year ago by stray dogs, last night I dreamed that all my chickens were back, roosting in odd places and scolding me for my inattention. In the same dream, a young friend I worry about for his reckless living of late, showed up hiding in a bushel of root vegetables, and not looking at all that out of place. I can easily attribute both these images to the codeine cough medicine I'm using to dose my cold. But I also suspect a part of my brain is wondering just what the outdoors is up to out here on the farm while I'm "cooped-up" inside.

Seriously, though, these old, cold days mark one of my favorite times of year, the time between the arrival of the seed catalogs and that odd February day when, if the ice isn't too slick or the snow too deep, we can slip out the back door, scratch a little line in some bare garden soil, and plant peas. It's the "Not Yet" time when every green thumb is itching for a little dirt to poke a seed into. But not yet. So what can we do to make the hours go faster, the nights to shorten, the clock hands to magically slip ahead?

I recommend more dreaming. Asleep or awake, it's only in dreams that I'll be able to feed those chickens, or ask Billy what the hell he's doing in my basket of beets. Or maybe I'll wander down some other road, Visit the Might-Be's, or the Coulda-Beens, or some new neighborhood altogether. No tickets required. No expense. Just the investment of the time it takes to find a quiet space, maybe by the fire, still your busy mind and put today on hold. It'll wait, and chances are good you'll find something out there in the land of Nod that will make you smile, give you an image that speaks without words, or leave with you some truth to ponder. Don't worry. Your heart knows how to keep beating, the clock will keep ticking, and supper preparations will be right where you left them. Soon enough, everything will begin to speed up, crocuses will pop out and you'll wish you'd remembered to have the mower blade sharpened. But not yet. Not yet, there is still time for dreaming. Look around for a cozy spot. Settle back. You are getting very ---sleepy. This is Marideth Sisco, wishing you sweet dreams in the land of Not Yet, somewhere out there in these Ozarks Hills.

Author's note:
Sometime between this essay and the next, due to the congestion of a number of programs wanting the same time slot, this radio series was moved from the last Friday of the month to the first Friday of the next month. Hence, the next episode, which once would have run on the last Friday of February, actually ran in the first Friday of March.

FEBRUARY/MARCH: To the Garden, at Last

Well, despite the date on the calendar it must be spring because the weather has been all over the place. Everything from tornados to daffodils, and we're just turning the corner from February into March. By my count, spring is three weeks ahead of schedule, and I haven't even ordered all my seeds yet. So I find myself saying a phrase that is no doubt being uttered right now by everybody in the Ozarks who grows a garden. 'I've gotta get a move on."

Easy to say. And the minute I said it this week, I went straight to some joke the old folks used to say about my get-up-and go having got up and gone, and that called into memory a poem that my Granny Gentry sent to my Aunt Juanita many years ago when Granny was in the Ozark hills of Missouri and her daughter Juanita was out in California working. Juanita found it so touching she copied it into the back of her cookbook for safekeeping. These many years later, when some folks look at my grey head and think I'm the old folks, the cookbook with the poem has come to me. You may also remember the poem. Granny's version goes like this:

When I was young, my slippers were red.
and I could kick my heels up over my head.
When I grew older, my slippers were blue,
but I could still dance the whole night through.

Now I am old. My slippers are black.
I walk to the corner and puff my way back.
But in spite of all that, I'm able to grin
when I think of where all my "get-up" has been!

182

There are many versions, one even made into a song by Pete Seeger. All of them written by Anonymous. All of them referencing the dilemma of age, and how the older one gets, and the more one settles on the activities and interests that are the most, well, interesting to them, the less energy one can muster for the pursuit. Take gardening, for instance. This last week, in a bit of a dry spell, I had my garden worked up by a kind friend with a tiller, and over the weekend I turned it into a tidy little patch of raised beds. They're not as wide as they used to be because I can't reach as far as I used to, But they'll do. And if I can get my back to bend a few more times, all those rocks I tossed to the grassy edges will go on my driveway where they belong.

Come summer, all that work will be done and it'll just be the heat and the bugs and the heat and the watering and the heat to contend with. But not yet. Spring, on this warming planet, may be upon us ahead of time. But summer is still a ways off, and winter could return at any moment, or not. Meanwhile there is work to be done. Slow work for me, with rest stops. But good work nonetheless, and welcome after a season of sloth. As I saw and hammer and nail together the rude boxes where soil will be sifted and amended and made friendly for carrots and other root veggies, my back kindly calls to my attention that the garden doesn't have nearly enough benches. So while I hammer and saw and try to convince myself not to plant the beans yet because it's too early, I'll be looking for shady spots with the best view, just right for a bench. Most people would say, and some already have, that it's too much work for a person of my years, that I should be taking it easy, and buy my beans at the store. But they evidently don't remember the taste of beans, corn and potatoes fresh from the garden. There's nothing that compares. I'm preparing for a season of gourmet fare, the kind the 99% can only afford if they grow it. We in the Ozarks have known this since way before anyone started counting the costs in percentages. And besides, this is the best of all times to be outdoors after the long dark days. The work, in fact, is merely the excuse to get out and, frankly, away from everything else that needs doing. Right now I'm in what might best be described as an ecstatic state, finding that particular joy that comes from escaping into my work, just as I do when I sing a song or write a line. And I relish being older. The truth is, I am finally old enough to recognize that life is not about recreation, but creation itself. Doing is sometimes the very best of being. Planting a row of peas is a splendid ritual. Hoeing corn and hilling up potatoes are meditations of the best sort.

Might I suggest, in fact, a short meditation on how it is that many so-called labor saving devices advertised as being created to give us the gift of leisure only ended up serving to put somebody, sometimes us, out of a job.

So this is what it's like getting old, at least today. So what if my hair has turned gray from all this thinking and doing. So what if my back requires both yoga and a pill or two to get all the way through the day in the garden. It's a glorious day any day I can put my hands or my heart or my imagination to work, and best when it involves all three. This isn't some kind of new-age practice or me going through a sudden manic phase. It's merely that little smidge of wisdom as sometimes comes to us old hillbillies, if we live long enough. It's not a new notion. Just an old one still worth celebrating by those of us who've survived long enough to appreciate it. As that wise hillbilly sage, Anonymous, said in another poem from long ago:

My Grandmother on a winter's day
Milked the cows and fed them hay
Slopped the hogs, saddled the mule
And got the children off to school;

Did a washing, mopped the floors
Washed the windows, and did some chores
Cooked a dish of home-dried fruit
Pressed her husband's Sunday suit

Swept the parlor, made the bed

Baked a dozen loaves of bread,
Split some firewood, and lugged it in,
Enough to fill the kitchen bin

Cleaned the lamps and put in oil,
Stewed some apples she thought would spoil
Cooked a supper that was delicious
And afterwards, washed up all the dishes

Fed the cat and sprinkled the clothes
Mended a basketful of hose;
Then opened the organ and began to play
"When you come to the end of a perfect day"

This is Marideth Sisco, in the midst of another perfect day in
These Ozarks Hills.

APRIL: Seasons Out of Kilter

I'm wondering today if anyone is having as much trouble with the calendar as I am. I spent most of mid-April this year in my garden, only it was the middle of March. Now April has come, and the May apples are up and blooming. Now don't get me wrong. I'm not pining away for the frost and the cold. But I've got to tell you, this out-of-season spring seems almost as alien to me as the one a few years back that waited until all the fruit was blooming and then hit us with three days of temps in the teens. That, of course, was as hideous as this year has been delightful. But alien still. And just as out of kilter.

I know that a good many folks may flinch and grab their pitchforks at the very mention of the phrase "global warming." So let's consider it unmentionable. But whatever's happening with the climate, I don't like it. I didn't like it when the armadillos got here. I didn't like it when the collared doves arrived, either, beautiful as they are. I got to know them down south on the Gulf while searching the sky and the trees for what might be making a noise like a crow with the croup. I thought they were interesting. But I'd never seen or heard them in the Ozarks before. But they're here now, and getting more common by the day.

And what am I to do in the garden? The peas are up and blooming, but some people are planting tomatoes, a month too soon. Gardens are always a gamble – too cold and the beans will rot, too hot, and the lettuce will bolt. But this spring, this month, belongs in Mississippi, not the Ozarks. I repeat. It's a charming devil, but I don't like it.

It could be worse, I know. The news tells of places on the globe where whole nations and their populations are getting blown or washed away. One Pacific Island nation recently voted to disband and move elsewhere before the island disappeared completely. Desertification is a word that I have no memory of from my childhood. It, too, is becoming commonplace.

Now don't go all politics on me and accuse me of going green. I'm just going Ozarks, as I always do, and wondering if the changes I see are fleeting or here to stay. And my answer to the situation, if it needs an answer, is to simply hold fast to the ways we in the Ozarks have always responded to changes, especially difficult changes.

Grow my garden so there's plenty in the pantry and freezer come fall. Choose my purchases wisely, so as to have what I need, and not what I'm persuaded by my television that I simply can't do without. I can do very well without a great deal of it, actually. Buy things that last, that are not disposable, and remember that none of my income is "disposable."

Continue to use, and value, the tools at hand, and if one needs replacing, buy the very best I can afford. Don't be too proud to visit stores that sell the pre-owned, as they say about used cars. This isn't just a way to get through hard times – it's a way of life, being frugal, living sparely and making choices mindfully.

Life is rarely expressed in the most meaningful terms by phrases that will fit on a bumper sticker. But there is one I saw some years back that spoke to me, and I have not forgotten it. It was a statement about wastefulness, and it said "Live Simply, that others may simply live."

It had a powerful effect on me at the time, because I was struggling to find a way to reconcile my frugal Ozarks ways, referred to by some as being "tight," or Scotch, with the profligate habits of those around me. I was living in Southern California at the time, a society that seemed to pride itself on its carefree lifestyle. All well and good, but it was astonishing to me, and not in a good way, how quickly the notion of being free of care translated into an outward urge to demonstrate that nothing mattered. Like the Beatles song, Strawberry Fields: Nothing is real. Nothing to get hung about. I just could never square that with my lifelong training of "use it up, wear it out, make it do or do without."

So I had to come home, and find a corner of the Ozarks where that saying and the way of life it proposes was still practiced. I found the notion a little frayed in the cities, a little tattered in the up-and-coming communities, but still intact, still recognized as not just an old way to be but a very ethical way to be - living as though everything matters. It's still a good idea, in these times or in any, in your comfort zone or somewhere in some alien spring. This is Marideth Sisco, celebrating, with some trepidations, a Mississippi Spring in these Ozark Hills.

MAY: Not Exactly Memory Lane

You'd think, that with May Day just past, I'd be telling you a May Day story. And someday I will. But other things have been cooking in this overcooked hillbilly brain, and so I've wandered off, and now I'm taking you with me. This is no doubt another age-related post, but as I'm fairly age-related myself, I guess you'll just have to bear with me.

Here's the thing. I've been doing some traveling lately on various errands, not all of them health related, but some, and have found myself doing some rather lengthy stints in the car alone. Radio reception, even with all the hard work KSMU does to maintain it, is not always the best through the ups and downs of the watersheds, and so there are periods of quiet, left to one's own thoughts.

It was in the middle of one of those periods, when taking a trip down what we're prone to calling Memory Lane, that I suddenly realized that on this trip I was not in fact on Memory Lane, but somewhere just south of Memory Swamp, near Memory Crag, and not all that far from Memory precipice. Not a good place to end up on a chilly, cloudy day, as I discovered while driving into the desolate village of Lament.

But then I had to admit while rounding the corner from Wistful to Wisteria gone Wild that such a destination is not nearly such a bad place while driving through the Springtime Ozarks as when trying to fall back to sleep after a dream of a lost loved one, or chewing the elderly bones of resentment over someone who once promised you the moon, when they did not in fact Have the moon.

Yes, it's true. The older you get, the more you amass collections of stuff in your memory basement to dig up and worry over at odd moments, especially when the time for doing anything that could change or better the outcome is long past.

There was that kid who broke my favorite cudgel (a knobby branch I found useful in the days of no friends at a new school, useful both as a toy and a weapon as needed). It wasn't that he disarmed me that's made me remember it for 60-some years.

it was that he laughed about it.

Then there was the friend who betrayed a trust, and then had the nerve to die without making amends. On the opposite end and always available to chew on is my own long ago casual thoughtlessness that wounded a friend and is still unhealed.

And as always, all those acts in the arrogance of youth that counted friendships less important than winning. The list goes on.

But then so does the spring day, and eventually the sun came out and I arrived home and headed out to the garden. And somewhere in the solitude of the garden, where I often go to get my hands in the reality of earth, I made my way back to the present tense, where I have landed more or less intact after my journey through regrets and remorse, I have come to make peace, if not with others, at least with myself.

It is here, I find, that other memories surface. Picking boatloads of yellow squash that my mother dredged in cornmeal and served with potatoes and okra in summer.

Walking down a country lane full of waving grasses, Queen Anne's Lace and Black-eyed Susans to my cousin Janice's house in hopes her mother was making what she called garden goulash, a stew of fresh tomatoes, onions, macaroni and ground beef, served with green beans with potatoes and bacon, sliced tomatoes and sweet corn.

From there it's a short hop to the summer I helped my aunt Juanita harvest apricots and Belle of Georgia peaches from her trees in California early in the morning of another 100-degree day, biting into a peach for breakfast and having the juice pour over my chin and down my arms to the elbows. The bees loved my elbows almost as much as the peaches.

No laments can come here except for times long gone and never forgotten, times of food, friendship and an intense, heartfelt joy that springs up unannounced, like rhubarb. Many religions say the garden is as close to God's heart as you can get. It would be hard to argue that life began anywhere else. A garden feeds you and your family. Gardens, in plural, feed the world. But they are more than a factory to fill the stomach. They also feed the soul, ease heart's pain, and heal the weary traveler, whatever the journey, either at its end or as a stop along the road. Here, every act is an act of faith, trusting the bean to always be a bean and not a tomato, trusting the sun not to sear and the rain to be plentiful and on time, setting plants out to grow for the sheer joy of watching it happen.

And as you grow older, it is also a growing awareness that one day you may be planting fruit that someone else may harvest, and trees under whose shade you may never sit. There's nothing wrong with that. It's our investment in the eternal, our participation in the passage of seasons. Plant. Grow. Harvest. Repeat. Good advice, for the garden and the gardener. This is Marideth Sisco, for the gardens and the gardeners in These Ozarks Hills.

badly bruised - силно наранен
(bru:s)

have a fit - имам припадък.

committed - (kamited) - ангажирам

Made in the USA
Charleston, SC
27 April 2014